Junior Handbook I

Alan Brighouse/David Godber/Peter Patilla

MATHEMATICS DEPT.
  S. Martins College

Nelson

Contents

trp   this symbol indicates the appropiate
sheet in the Teacher's Resource Pack

Thomas Nelson and Sons Ltd
Nelson House   Mayfield Road
Walton-on-Thames   Surrey KT12 5PL   UK

51 York Place
Edinburgh
EH1 3JD   UK

Thomas Nelson (Hong Kong) Ltd
Toppan Building 10/F   22A Westlands Road
Quarry Bay   Hong Kong

Distributed in Australia by

Thomas Nelson Australia
480 La Trobe Street   Melbourne   Victoria 3000
and in Sydney, Brisbane, Adelaide and Perth

© **A. Brighouse, D. Godber, P. Patilla 1984**

First published by Thomas Nelson and Sons Ltd 1984

ISBN 0-17-421364-6

NPN 9 8 7 6 5

Printed in Hong Kong

Filmset in the Nelson Teaching Alphabet
by Mould Type Foundry Ltd
Dunkirk Lane   Leyland   England

General Introduction

On transfer from the Infants to the Junior School, some children will still need the later work outlined in Infant Handbook 2; others will already have started working from the early pupils' books. This handbook details the content of Peak Books 0 to 4 commenting upon specific teaching points where appropriate. It also suggests chapter by chapter, further activities to supplement or extend skills being developed.

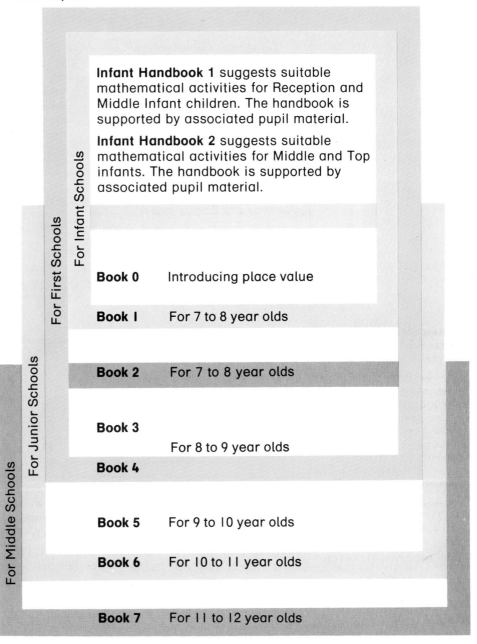

For First Schools

For Infant Schools

Infant Handbook 1 suggests suitable mathematical activities for Reception and Middle Infant children. The handbook is supported by associated pupil material.

Infant Handbook 2 suggests suitable mathematical activities for Middle and Top infants. The handbook is supported by associated pupil material.

Book 0   Introducing place value

Book 1   For 7 to 8 year olds

Book 2   For 7 to 8 year olds

Book 3

For Junior Schools

For Middle Schools

              For 8 to 9 year olds

Book 4

Book 5   For 9 to 10 year olds

Book 6   For 10 to 11 year olds

Book 7   For 11 to 12 year olds

The early part of the Infant Scheme is organised into four consecutive sections within two Infant Handbooks—Infant Handbook 1 and Infant Handbook 2, with the work on Number in the second Handbook supported by 232 children's workcards on Number, 112 on Measurement and 64 on Money. After Section 4 the format alters in that the materials are presented in the form of pupils' text books.

Record sheets are provided so that the teacher can monitor each child's progress.

Record sheet Sections 3 and 4

Name

Date of birth

Date record started

School

Class

peak mathematics

Section 3

Number   *Numbers up to 10*   Card Nos.

Stage 1 Number groups		Stage 5 Partitioning	
Counting and recording	1–1 to 1–5 ☐	Partitioning of a group	1–1 to 1–4 ☐
Sub-division of groups	2–1 to 2–5 ☐	**Stage 6 Subtraction**	
Comparison of groups	3–1 to 3–5 ☐	Using real objects	1–1 to 1–5 ☐
Stage 2 One-to-one correspondence		Pictorially	2–1 to 2–5 ☐
Comparison for equality	1–1 to 1–5 ☐	Language (less than)	3–1 to 3–5 ☐
Comparison for inequality	2–1 to 2–10 ☐	Language (take away)	4–1 to 4–5 ☐
Stage 3 Seriation		Subtraction bonds	5–1 to 5–5 ☐
Number symbols	1–1 to 1–4 ☐	**Stage 7 Complementary addition**	
Number words	2–1 to 2–4 ☐	By counting on	1–1 to 1–6 ☐
Stage 4 Combining groups		**Stage 8 Addition**	
Pictorially	1–1 to 1–5 ☐	In various formats	1–1 to 1–10 ☐
Pictorially (recorded with symbols)	2–1 to 2–5 ☐	**Stage 9 Subtraction**	
Using structured apparatus	3–1 to 3–5 ☐	In various formats	1–1 to 1–10 ☐
Using number symbols	4–1 to 4–5 ☐	**Stage 10 Number line**	
Language of addition	5–1 to 5–5 ☐	Number line (0–50)	☐
By mapping	6–1 to 6–5 ☐		
Addition bonds	7–1 to 7–5 ☐		

Shape   Recognition of square, circle, rectangle, triangle ☐   Recognition of cube, sphere, cylinder, cuboid ☐

Measurement   Use of an arbitrary unit to measure objects

Length	1–1 to 1–3 ☐	2–1 to 2–3 ☐	3–1 to 3–3 ☐
	4–1 to 4–3 ☐	5–1 to 5–3 ☐	6–1 to 6–3 ☐
	7–1 to 7–3 ☐	8–1 to 8–3 ☐	9–1 to 9–7 ☐
Weight	1–1 to 1–3 ☐	2–1 to 2–3 ☐	3–1 to 3–3 ☐
	4–1 to 4–3 ☐	5–1 to 5–3 ☐	6–1 to 6–3 ☐
Capacity	1–1 to 1–3 ☐	2–1 to 2–3 ☐	3–1 to 3–3 ☐
	4–1 to 4–3 ☐	5–1 to 5–3 ☐	

Can estimate sensibly

Length ☐   Weight ☐   Capacity ☐

Money   Equivalence and addition of coins up to 10p ☐

Time   General calendar work ☐

Graphs   Picture graphs – compilation ☐

© Brighouse, Godber, Patilla   Thomas Nelson and Sons Limited   ISBN 0-17-421322-0   NCN 0661-13-0

You will see from the diagram on page 3 that there is an overlap between the Infant and the Junior school materials. This overlap is quite deliberate for we feel that where such schools exist separately it is inevitable that some children may well progress beyond the point where slower children in the Junior School begin. Similar comment also relates to the transition between the First and Middle Schools where an overlap is also indicated.

The broad areas of mathematics applicable to the Juniors are shown on the matrix on pages 12 to 14.

Introduction to the Junior part of the scheme

In the Junior part of the scheme there is a provision of two books per year for the 7 to 8 year olds and the 8 to 9 year olds (Books 1 and 2, Books 3 and 4). For a child using mathematics textbooks in the early years we feel it is preferable to break each year's work into two consecutive books. Apart from the extra flexibility this allows in organisation within the classroom, no child will be overwhelmed by the amount of work to be faced at any stage. Books 1 to 4 are shorter than the later books, and may well be covered in a much shorter time.

Curriculum

Number   During the course of Infant experience, the child should have acquired the appropriate language and symbolism of Number work, and developed a very sound understanding of numbers up to 20 and number bond work in all its forms. He should also have a knowledge of numbers up to 100 as a result of Number line and associated activities.

The main emphasis initially in the Junior part of the scheme is on place value work, which is carefully introduced by the use of structured apparatus before the child proceeds to the formal operations of Number. Activities involving multi-base structured apparatus, other than denary, have not been formally included in the scheme for the teaching of place value, although it is recognised that they can be beneficial. However, notes on the use of multi-base materials for this purpose can be found on page 15, and where the suggested activities are incorporated, they should be done prior to Book 0. Book 0 concerns itself with activities relating to place value and the understanding of the denary system. Once this has been established, the formal operations are introduced in a most carefully graded way and each new step of the different processes is supported by practical experience, and thoroughly understood before being applied. In Subtraction, for instance, a great deal of attention has been paid to the various stages of decomposition before the child is asked to apply the operation.

In each formal operation, there are three general stages to be considered:
1. The understanding of the operation.
2. The acquisition of the skill.
3. The application of the skill to problem solving.

The scheme provides a thorough grounding in the first stage before requiring the child to tackle Stages 2 and 3.

Work on Money runs alongside that on Number, and similar care has been taken to ensure that an understanding of the monetary system is acquired. By the end of Book 4, the child should be able to understand and apply the formal operations in Number and Money and the later books are concerned with their application to problems of all types.

The Fraction work is developed from early activities of a practical nature illustrating the equivalences involved. Once these equivalences have been appreciated, the later books offer a wide range of experiences involving fractions, including computation.

The scheme provides a substantial amount of computation and problem work and extra provision in the form of "more practice" pages (apart from Book 6 and Book 7) for those children for whom the teacher feels extra work is needed.

Measurement   Early experiences in Measurement involved the child in conservation activities from which precise language and the eventual need of units of measurement were derived. At such an early age, the standard units of measurement are most unsuitable and it was necessary, therefore, to involve the child in activities which afforded him measuring experience, but with a whole range of personal and arbitrary units (e.g. spans, cupfuls, ribbons, etc.) which are more suitable for his use. This work should have extended his language of measurement and he should have acquired experience in the following:

1. Estimation—an indication that he appreciates the value of the units being used.
2. Choice of arbitrary units—an indication that he is able to choose sensible units for different tasks.
3. Approximation—an indication that he appreciates the level of precision required for particular tasks.

At this stage, the child is ready for experience with standard units, such experience being of a practical nature initially (Book 1), and the aims outlined in connection with the early work should still be borne in mind all through the early work with standard units. Eventually the need for computational skills in measurement arises naturally, and each is carefully introduced with the relationship between the various units clearly established. As the child acquires the relevant skills he is then ready for the opportunity to apply them in solving problems, some of which will be of a practical and environmental nature.

Time   By the time the child enters Junior school, he should be familiar with the general vocabulary of time (e.g. days of week, months, the calendar, etc.), and the major intervals of time (e.g. o'clock, $\frac{1}{4}$ past, $\frac{1}{2}$ past, $\frac{1}{4}$ to). In the Junior part of the scheme, the oral and written notation of time is developed, and this work is extended to include work on the 24 hour clock and its application to timetables.

Spatial relationships Early experiences with shapes should have enabled the child to recognise and name the simple regular plane and solid shapes.

The child is now ready to explore the properties of regular and irregular shapes and develop fundamental concepts of geometry. The ideas on shape and angles in the scheme work systematically and enjoyably towards this end.

Graphs The idea of pictorial representation should be understood by the child as a result of compilation and interpretation of picture graphs by classes at Infant level.

This idea is extended to column graphs without the complication of difficult scales in Book I, and then is systematically developed through the scheme, with each new type of graph and scale carefully introduced, drawn and interpreted. Attention is paid to the need for adequate and correct labelling, as well as to the need of choosing the most appropriate type of graph and suitable scale.

Content within the books

The scheme is so designed as to allow maximum flexibility in its use within the classroom, and to permit each child, or group of children, to proceed at an appropriate pace without interfering with the progress of others. A broad outline of the planning within the books is shown below, and further suggestions concerning the possible use in the classroom are shown in the detailed notes on each book.

Book 0 This book deals with place value work leading to the formal operation of addition of Number, and needs to be worked through in a linear fashion before attempting Book I. It demands of the child, initially, a sound understanding of number bond work up to 20, and proceeds to develop an appreciation of place value through the use of structured apparatus.

As the understanding of the denary system and the equivalences involved takes place, the formal operation of addition is introduced in order to ensure that the child can apply the principles of place value. Other formal number operations are introduced in later books.

Assessment pages are included at the end of the book to test whether the teaching points have been understood.

Books I to 7 In Books I to 4, the contents of each book are divided into chapters, each relating to one of the four major areas of mathematics, namely Number, Measurement, Spatial Relationships and Graphs. The exception to this is the chapter (or chapters) in each book called "Investigations", which includes open-ended situations of a more demanding kind than may be found elsewhere in the books.

The chapters within each book may be done in any order. Each chapter is independent and will not involve concepts developed elsewhere in the same book. However, each concept developed in a book will be exploited fully in the following book. Hence the need to complete each book before proceeding to the next one. We hope that with this flexibility, teachers may not be restricted in their organisation of the mathematics lesson, and that the facility for grouping and regrouping of children, if desired, may be heightened.

The work within each chapter, is, of course, progressive, and it is essential that once a chapter is started, the child works sequentially through it. This is equally true of chapters relating to the formal operations of number, where the examples are carefully graded in order of difficulty and are based on the levels of skill that have been acquired at each stage.

In Books 5 to 7, the work on each main area of mathematics is spread through the book and is often of a more general nature. This ensures that a child working consecutively through the pages will be involved in a variety of mathematical activities.

The apparatus required for each activity/operation is shown at the top of each page. This apparatus should be assembled beforehand so that it is readily available to the children. An apparatus list, showing the total requirements of each book, is shown on page 142.

Books 0 to 5 contain sections which will enable teachers to provide extra computational practice for those children who require it.

At the end of each book is a glossary of new terms introduced in that book which can be used as a valuable point of reference.

The care with which the scheme has been written ensures a sound mathematical development for the child working through it. This relieves the teacher to a large extent of the problem of planning such a course and providing all the ideas required. However, the scheme depends upon the teacher being actively involved, at all stages; with the implementation of it; through good organisational planning; effective marking; assessment and relevant discussion with each child or group of children. The scheme also allows teachers to supplement the material by the development of the suggested activities outlined in this book, and by the incorporation of environmental mathematics, where appropriate. Indeed, it in no way precludes teachers from adding their own material as they see fit.

Providing supplementary materials

The main stages of mathematical development in Peak mathematics are outlined earlier in this book, and activities designed to ensure a child's progress through those stages are to be found in the pupils' materials. However it cannot be emphasised too strongly that the success of the scheme depends upon the teacher's involvement, both in the teaching of the skills and the provision, where necessary, of supplementary material. The use of the scheme as the mainstream of mathematical development for each child in no way precludes the inclusion of material from other sources, and especially any provided by the teacher or school. However, thought must be given to the content of supplementary materials, to ensure that it fits in with the skills so far acquired by the child.

As stated earlier in this book, there are three main stages of development for each new skill introduced in Peak mathematics:

Stage 1—Understanding of the process and language being introduced.

Stage 2—Abstraction of computational skill.

Stage 3—Application of the skill acquired to new situations.

Each of these stages may require the provision of supplementary materials for particular children, and certainly no child can be given too many opportunities to apply his skills to the solving of problems. In the provision of supplementary work at each stage, the following comments may be helpful:

Stage 1 Understanding of the process

At this stage, the main concern in providing supplementary materials is to allow extra work for any child who has had difficulty in understanding the process being introduced. It may be a case of presenting the same process or technique in a slightly different way practically. There may also be some children who simply need more experience than the books are able to provide, in order to consolidate this stage of learning.

Stage 2 Practice in computational skills

It is hoped that the amount of practice built into the pupils' materials, especially with the extra practice examples at the end of each of the earlier books, will be sufficient for most children. It is inevitable, however, that there will be some children who need yet further work; care must be taken that the skills included in such further work are in line with those that have in fact been developed. For instance it will confuse a child if, in giving him further practice in subtraction, "0" is inadvertently included on the top line before actual teaching of that situation has taken place.

It is probably stating the obvious to say that it is necessary to constantly revise all computational skills with children, and here again the teacher plays an important role in ensuring that no skills which have already been taught, are forgotten.

Stage 3 Application of skills

At this stage supplementary work provided by the teacher is vital. It falls into two categories.

1. Extra work aimed at the application of taught skills to a whole range of new situations, many of which will be based on the immediate environment of the school. Although the later books in the scheme present an increasing amount of work in this category, they can never offer more than a very limited amount of work specifically related to a child's own school, or to topics being developed across the curriculum.

2. Extra work aimed at the further development of taught skills, especially by the use of investigatory activities. Again the later books include an increasing number of such activities, but it is hoped that further work will be added by the teacher.

When providing work for both aspects of Stage 3, some, or all, of the following demands should be made on a child, during each task:

a) to decide on the most appropriate unit to use, especially if measurement work is involved.
b) to decide on the level of precision or approximation needed.
c) to take appropriate measurements.
d) to decide on the formal operation which is required.
e) to apply computational skills.
f) to record appropriately.

By a combination of some or all of these, the problem posed can be solved.

Since most of the development of computational skills takes place in the early years of the Primary School, it follows that most of the supplementary work provided in the first two years of the Junior School will be concerned with Stages 1 and 2. As the child progresses through the school, the amount of supplementary work for Stage 3 will increase, and, indeed, it is the child's ability to deal with the work involved at this stage of his development, which indicates whether his previous teaching has been effective.

It is hoped that the "further activities" suggested in the Handbook will help you to provide some of the necessary supplementary activities for each child.

Computer software, designed to test the child's ability to apply his acquired skills to real situations, is available for use alongside the Peak materials.

Testing

Mathematics testing in school takes many different forms and it is important that thought is given to the specific purpose of the tests we administer, and the content we include. Much testing is ongoing and done incidentally by teachers; indeed, with a structured approach to mathematics, each time a child applies his skills to new situations his expertise is being tested. However, in the more formal situations, whether it be a class test set by the teacher or a commercial test, it is sensible to consider the content in some detail, to ensure that the purpose of the test is clear.

Perhaps before looking directly at actual test content, it would be helpful to first consider the structured development built into the Peak materials. Throughout the scheme, for each new skill area to which a child is introduced he is given:

1. practical experience to develop understanding of the process and language involved, leading to:
2. the abstraction and practice of computational skills, leading to:
3. the application of the experience gained, and the skills acquired, to a new mathematical situation.

These stages also pertain to testing, and the questions within tests can be summarised into four categories as follows:

1. Questions to test understanding of processes (place value, decomposition, finding area etc.).
2. Questions to test computational skills (arithmetic).
3. Questions to test factual recall (names of shapes etc.).
4. Questions to test ability to apply skills to new problems.

The assessment tests built into the Peak materials concentrate heavily on categories 1, 2 and 3 in order to establish that the skills and language developed in each book are sufficiently understood for further development and application. A child's ability to apply his acquired skills (category 4) will be continuously tested by the content of subsequent books.

Tests prepared by teachers for their own use should ideally contain questions in all the four categories, unless they are specifically intended to test one particular area (e.g. tables test). The balance of content between the four categories in tests will change as a child progresses through the school. In the lower junior years the balance will lean towards categories 1 and 2; at the top of the Junior school the balance will be more evenly distributed.

Standardised tests are available for 8 to 12 year olds which, as well as giving individual scores, show a child's performance in each of the categories of questions outlined above. These are marketed by NFER Nelson and are called **Mathematics 8 to 12**.

Infant/Junior Scheme Matrix

	Section 4	Book 0
Number		
Place Value		Place value, Tens, Units Place value, Hundreds, Tens, Units
Addition	Number bonds up to 20 Various formats	Addition, Tens, Units Addition, Hundreds, Tens, Units
Subtraction	Number bonds up to 20 Various formats difference	
Multiplication	Early ideas of multiplication (practical)	
Division	Early ideas of division (practical)	
Money	Equivalence of coins up to 50 Addn/Subn up to 50p	
Fractions		
General	Number line activities up to/over 100	
Measurement		
Length		
Weight	Activities involving a choice of arbitrary units	
Capacity		
Area		
Time	Telling the time	
Spatial relationships		
Shape	Revision of plane and solid shapes	
Angles		
Graphs	Picture graphs	
Investigations		
More practice		

Book 1	Book 2
Addition – various formats Hundreds, Tens, Units	Addition – various formats Thousands, Hundreds, Tens, Units
Subtraction, Tens, Units – no decomposition (initially using structured apparatus)	Subtraction, Hundreds, Tens, Units (with decomposition)
Subtraction Tens, Units – with decomposition (initially using structured apparatus) Repeated addition of 2 up to 20 Repeated addition of 5 up to 50 Repeated addition of 10 up to 100	
	Compilation of 2, 5, 10, 3, 4, 6, tables Multiplication by 2, 5, 10, 3, 4, 6
Simple sharing of Tens, Units – no decomposition (using structured apparatus)	Sharing Tens, Units – with decomposition (using structured apparatus)
Equivalence and addition of coins up to £1 Subtraction of coins up to 50p	Introduction of £ notation Addition and subtraction in £ notation
Introduction of $\frac{1}{2}$ introduction of $\frac{1}{4}$ (practically – to show equivalence to whole one)	Introduction of $\frac{3}{4}$ Equivalence of $\frac{1}{4}$, $\frac{1}{2}$, $\frac{3}{4}$, whole one
Estimating and measuring in cm	
Introduction of the gram – balancing with grams	Introduction of m notation Addition of m notation Estimating and weighing in g Addition of g
Introduction of the litre – use of litre measure to fill other containers	Equivalence of litre, $\frac{1}{2}$ litre, $\frac{1}{4}$ litre
Introduction of minutes past notation Minutes in one hour	Telling the time – minutes past notation
Naming of plane shapes (with tessellating activities). Naming of solid shapes. Introduction of cone and triangular prism	Faces, edges, vertices of solid shapes. Plane shape in solid shape. Introduction of hexagon
	Turning – $\frac{1}{4}$ turn, $\frac{1}{2}$ turn, full turn Clockwise, anti-clockwise
Introduction of column graphs (Scale 1:1)	Column graphs – introduction of scale 1:2
Properties of number Geoboard activities	Geoboard activities Properties of number Pegboard activities
Addition of number, Hundreds, Tens, Units Subtraction of number, Tens, Units, Problems	Addition of Thousands, Hundreds, Tens, Units Subtraction of Thousands, Hundreds, Tens, Units Multiplication of Tens and Units by 2, 3, 4, 5, 6, 10 Addition, subtraction of £ notation Addition of m notation Addition of g Problems

Infant/Junior Scheme Matrix

	Book 3	Book 4
Number		
Place Value		
Addition	Addition – various formats Thousands, Hundreds, Tens, Units	Addition – various formats Thousands, Hundreds, Tens, Units Quick addition of 99
Subtraction	Subtraction, Thousands, Hundreds, Tens, Units	Subtraction, Thousands, Hundreds, Tens, Units Quick subtraction of 99
Multiplication	Compilation of 7, 8, 9 tables Multiplication of Hundreds, Tens, Units, by single integers and 10	Multiplication of Thousands, Hundreds, Tens, Units Quick multiplication by 10
Division	Division of Hundreds, Tens, Units (no remainders)	Division of Thousands, Hundreds, Tens, Units (with remainders) Quick division by 10
Money	Addition, subtraction and multiplications of money	Addition, Subtraction, Multiplication and Division
Fractions	Introduction of $\frac{1}{3}$ Finding $\frac{1}{4}$, $\frac{1}{3}$, $\frac{1}{2}$ of quantities	Introduction of $\frac{1}{8}$ – equivalences involved
General	Odd and even numbers	Factors of numbers
Measurement		
Length	Addition and subtraction in m notation Introduction of perimeter	Addition, Subtraction, Multiplication and Division of length
Weight	Addition and subtraction of g Problems	Introduction of kg notation
Capacity	Estimating and measuring in ml	Introduction of litre notation
Area	Finding area by counting squares and $\frac{1}{2}$ squares	Introduction of cm² Area in cm²
Time	Introduction of am, pm	Introduction of minutes past/to the hour
Spatial relationships		
Shape	Introduction of line symmetry	Introduction of pentagon, octagon, equilateral triangle, family of quadrilaterals. Partition of plane shapes by diagonal diameter. Introduction of semicircle
Angles	Introduction of 4 points of compass Introduction of right angle, use of set square	Introduction of $\frac{1}{2}$ right angle Introduction to 8 points of compass
Graphs	Column graphs, introduction of scale 1:10	Column graphs – introduction of scale 1:100
Investigations	Tessellating tiles Magic squares Equaliser work Routes	Pentominoes Square numbers Pegboard activities Digital patterns
More practice	Addition of Thousands, Hundreds, Tens, Units Subtraction of Thousands, Hundreds, Tens, Units Multiplication of Hundreds, Tens, Units Division of Hundreds, Tens, Units (no remainders) Addition, Subtraction of money Addition, Subtraction of m, g Problems	Addition, Subtraction of number Multiplication, Division of number Computation of money Computation of length

The teaching of place value

In the Infant Section of this scheme, addition and subtraction bonds up to 20 were developed, and early ideas of division and multiplication were introduced. Before we can expect the child to manipulate large numbers, he must first understand the concept of place value. Some teachers may feel that this can best be achieved by the exclusive use of Base 10 structured apparatus, and where this is the case, it is suggested that the child progresses immediately to Book 0. However, others feel that the initial introduction to place value can beneficially be done by the use of structured materials in other bases, not in order to teach formal operations in those bases, but to illustrate equivalence of a number system with numbers within a child's counting ability. Where this is the case, the following notes will be useful in guiding a child through the various stages involved, before proceeding to Book 0.

The materials to use

Appropriate materials to use to show the equivalences involved in place value are Tillichs Blocks and Dienes Multibase Arithmetic Blocks (sometimes known as M.A.B. materials) which are both available from E. J. Arnold.

Base 3 materials

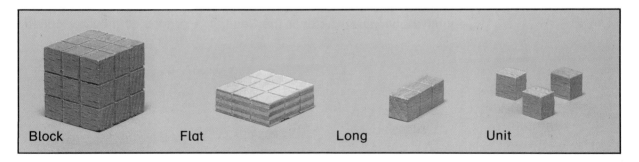

Block   Flat   Long   Unit

Base 5 materials

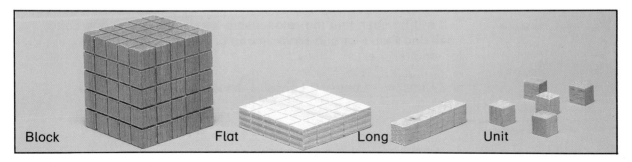

Block   Flat   Long   Unit

More of the smaller pieces of the apparatus (i.e. Units and Longs) are needed than the larger Flats and Blocks when doing place value work. It is sensible, therefore, to buy greater quantities of Units and Longs and not so many Flats and Blocks; where the apparatus is bought in "sets" you may find that you have insufficient of the small pieces and too many of the larger ones.

The bases to use

Since work with Base 2 materials is very limiting, it is suggested that the child works initially with Base 3 apparatus, before proceeding to similar activities with Base 5 materials. Having had experience with the equivalence of Base 3 and Base 5 materials respectively, he should be ready for the activities of Book 0, which are based on the denary system.

Materials in other bases could be used in addition to the ones suggested, but the advantage of using Base 3 and Base 5 materials lies in the fact that they offer plenty of experience of equivalence without involving difficult numbers.

Using Base 3 materials

In order to use a name for each piece of apparatus which will be equally applicable whatever the Base, it is suggested they are called:

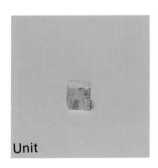
Unit

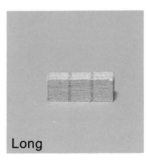
Long

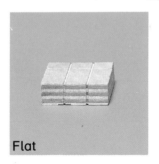
Flat

Block

It will be seen that the relationship between the Unit and Long, Long and Flat, Flat and Block is one of being 3 times larger (or smaller) i.e.

3 Units = 1 Long,   3 Longs = 1 Flat,   3 Flats = 1 Block

The activities listed below, which require the use of this apparatus, are designed to promote an understanding of that relationship for the child, and how it can be used to develop a number system. Through these activities the child will appreciate the equivalence involved in a number system, and the importance of the position of a digit in determining its value.

Stage I **Familiarisation with the apparatus**

If it is felt necessary, allow free play to "discover" the pieces. Children may build towers, bridges, etc.

Matching activities to learn the names of the pieces of apparatus.

Matching apparatus to pictures with names written alongside.

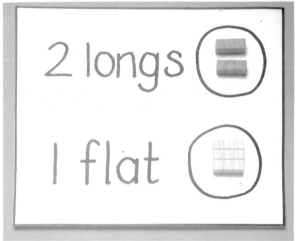

Matching apparatus to names.

Stage 2 Equivalence activities

The aim of these activities is for the child to appreciate the equivalences involved with the apparatus, i.e.

I Long $\longleftrightarrow$ 3 Units

I Flat $\longleftrightarrow$ 3 Longs $\longleftrightarrow$ 9 Units

I Block $\longleftrightarrow$ 3 Flats $\longleftrightarrow$ 9 Longs $\longleftrightarrow$ 27 Units

Establishing the equivalences involved between the various pieces of apparatus is best done by discussion with the child. Practical activities matching 3 Units to a Long, 3 Longs to a Flat, and so on are needed to show the equivalences of Base 3 apparatus. Once these equivalences are appreciated the child can then proceed to a more formal presentation.

The child puts the equivalent apparatus in the second circle (in this case 2 Longs). If he puts I Long and 3 Units in the second circle, this is acceptable as an equivalence, but the child needs prompting to replace the 3 Units for a further Long.

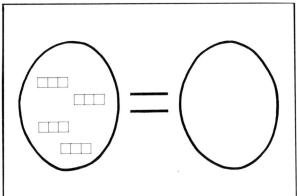

Similar work needs to be done on the upward conversion of other pieces of the apparatus.

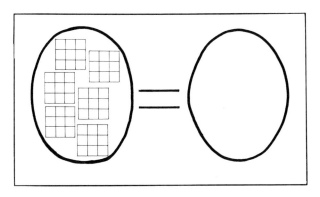

(Do not use more than 8 Flats for changing to Blocks, in order to avoid finishing with 3 Blocks or more.)

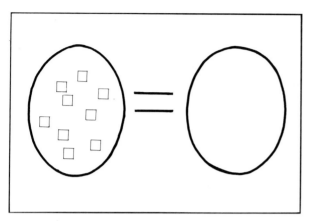

Increase the number of Units so that the child converts to Longs, but then can convert further to Flats. Eventually start with sufficient Units to enable the child to convert up to Blocks.

Eventually the child could be allowed to take a "handful" of apparatus to change up, although again it would be advisable to ensure that he never finished with more than 2 Blocks. (The next piece of apparatus in the sequence would be a Long Block, which it is sensible to avoid.)

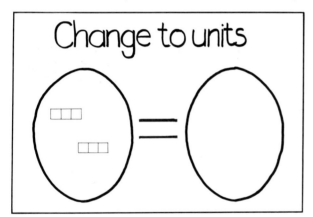

Similar work can be done converting the apparatus down to Units.

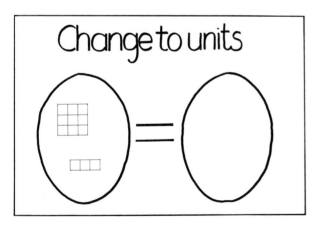

Equivalence chains

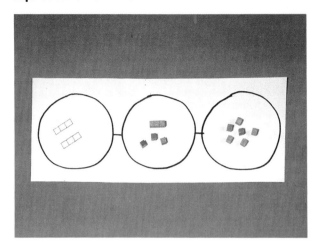

Child to place as many equivalences as he can think of in the chain. He can add to the chain if he wishes.
This work could be produced on large cards or worksheets.

Stage 3 Using equivalences to develop a number system

These activities help to develop the idea of a number system, based on the equivalences to which the child has been introduced. A place value sheet will be necessary, large enough to place the apparatus on, and made out of laminated stiff card for long life trP 15, 16.

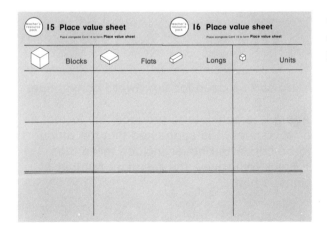

You will not require many of these place value sheets, since children will probably reach this stage at different times.

The child places the workcard (showing the number of Units to be changed) alongside the place value sheet and completes the conversion. It is suggested he does not start with more than 30 Units.

The child's recording can eventually be formalised into:

Put out	Change to B. F. L.U.
15 units	$\longrightarrow$
21 units	$\longrightarrow$
17 units	$\longrightarrow$
20 units	$\longrightarrow$

This format can be produced as a worksheet, with the child simply filling in the numbers.

Similar methods of recording can be used for downward conversion.

B. F. L.U.	Change to Units
2 0 1	$\longrightarrow$
1 0 0 2	$\longrightarrow$
22	$\longrightarrow$
1 1 0 0	$\longrightarrow$

Again it is sensible to produce this format as a worksheet. It is suggested that the amounts to be converted never include more than 1 Block, otherwise the resultant number of Units is high.

Stage 4   Using equivalence to combine 2 groups

At this stage the child is now familiar with the equivalences involved between the Units, Longs, Flats and Blocks of Base 3 apparatus.
In order to apply those equivalences it is sensible to present him with an addition situation to see whether he can operate them. This is not an attempt to make the child adept at addition in Base 3 (formal work in Bases will come much later, possibly at Secondary level); it is simply to ensure that the understanding of the equivalences with the Base 3 apparatus (i.e. place value) has taken place, so that it can be further extended.

When the child first tackles the addition work, the teacher needs to discuss and illustrate the process with him, using the place value sheet trp 15, 16

When combining the groups it is wise to start with the Units, convert as necessary, and then move on to the adding of the Longs, rather than bring all the apparatus into the answer box before doing any conversion. In this way the steps the child takes practically will be the same as those he follows when working in the abstract.

When the child is ready for formal recording, he should record each column as he completes the conversion practically. This is the method he will use at the abstract stage.

B.F.L.U.	B.F.L.U	B.F.L.U
1 0 2 1	2 0 1 2	1 0 1
+ 2 1 1	+ 2 2	+1 0 2 2

B.F.L.U	B.F.L.U	B.F.L.U
2 2 1	1 0 2 1	2 0 2
+1 0 2 2	+2 1 2	+ 1 2 1

The child can work from cards like this, or on worksheets. Ensure that the final answer does not result in three Blocks.

The addition, involving equivalence of Units → Longs → Flats → Blocks, may well be done eventually without apparatus.

During the course of the work with Base 3 apparatus, it is intended that the child becomes familiar with the principle of place value, and the equivalences involved in a number system. This is the sole aim of the work, and in order to further this aim, it is now sensible to consolidate by following a similar pattern with Base 5 materials.

Using Base 5 materials

The activities with Base 5 materials follow precisely the path detailed for Base 3 materials, but may well proceed faster for many children, since they are now familiar with the processes involved. As before it is hoped that the child will eventually appreciate that the position of a digit determines its value, and will understand the role of the digit "0".

It is anticipated that the work with the multi-base materials may take a few weeks, and it will be necessary, of course, to intersperse it with other mathematics activities from time to time. No work on subtraction has been included in these activities, although the principle of decomposition has been introduced, since it will be a little while before the child meets the process in his denary work. However, it is felt that the work with multi-base materials will enhance his eventual understanding of the denary system, and the materials should now be put away for the child to progress to Book 0, where he will use denary materials only.

Book 0

The aim of this book is to build upon the Number work which has already been done in the Infant Section and develop an understanding of the denary notation of number. The main emphasis, therefore, is on the understanding of place value and its application in the addition situation.

The following pages detail the content of each page of Peak Book 0 and where appropriate, include comments upon specific teaching points. It also suggests further activities which supplement, consolidate or extend the skills developed.

Book 0

Page no.	Content	New language
4–5	Revision of Number bonds	
6	Revision of Number line work	
7	Equivalence of Tens and Units	
8	Conversion of Units to Tens and Units	
9	Conversion of Tens and Units to Units	
10–11	Addition of Tens and Units (no conversion)	
12–13	Addition of Tens and Units (with conversion U → T)	
14	Recognition of numbers over 100; numbers from words to figures	
15	Introduction of a Hundred; equivalence of Hundreds and Tens	
16	Conversion of Tens to Hundreds and Tens	
17	Recognition of numbers shown by apparatus	
18	Addition of Hundreds, Tens, Units (with conversion T → H)	
19	Addition of Hundreds, Tens, Units (with conversion U → T, T → H)	
20–21	Addition of Hundreds, Tens, Units (with conversion U → T → H)	
22–23	Abacus work, involving hundreds	abacus, abaci
24	Numbers as words and figures	
25	Number patterns in addition	
26	Addition of Hundreds, Tens, Units (with conversion U → T)	
27	Addition of Hundreds, Tens, Units (with conversion T → H)	
28	Addition of Hundreds, Tens, Units (with conversion U → T → H)	
29	General addition—Hundreds, Tens, Units	
30–31	Assessment Test	

For those children who have already used multi-base materials for place value work, as explained on pages 15–17, the content of Book 0 is an extension of that work using denary apparatus. For those who have progressed immediately from the Infant workcards to Book 0, this will be their introduction to place value. In both cases a place value sheet, as illustrated on page 18 of Book 0, would be useful for the conversion and addition work in the book.

At each stage of the work in Book 0 the decision about when the child works without apparatus is a matter for your discretion.

Where addition is presented in horizontal format in this book, we expect the child to set the work down vertically, whether he is using apparatus or working abstractly. Guidance must be given to the child in the setting out of his work and especially where to put the carrying figure.

Further activities

Number recognition

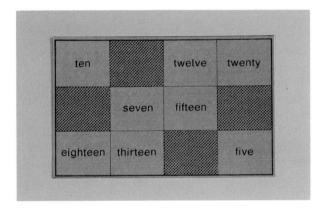

Lotto game: Each child in the group has one lotto board. The teacher writes random numbers up to 20 in digits, one number at a time, on a board. The first child to cover up all the number words with counters is the Winner *trp* 19, 20, 21, 22

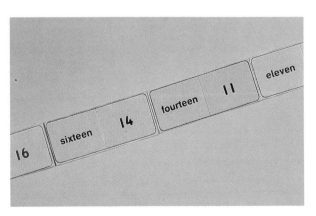

Number dominoes: Matching word numbers to digit numbers *trp* 23, 24

Number matching game: There are two piles of cards, one of number words and one of number symbols. A card from each pile is turned over by each child in turn. Any child who turns over two matching cards keeps them. *trp* 25, 26

The child is given a card with two or three numbers on, written in words.
He has to put the numbers on the calculator, pressing the + key between each and finally the = key.
The final answer is shown on the card, so the child can self-check whether he has entered the correct numbers.

Number facts

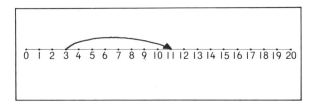

A number line is duplicated with an arrow drawn, the child is to write the operation on the arrow, in this case +8. Suitable for addition and subtraction facts. (Could be used later for multiplication and division facts also.) *trp* I.

Dice game:
a) Children playing in pairs. Each child starts with score of 30 and throws a dice. The number shown on the dice is subtracted from his score of 30. Children throw alternately—the first to reach 0 is the Winner.

b) The same game can be played, each starting with a score of 0, adding the score shown on the dice—first to reach 30 wins.

c) The game can be varied by having a score of 15 which relates to both players. One player throws the dice to add to that score (in order to try and reach 30); the other player throws to subtract from that score (in order to reach 0). Whoever reaches his objective first is the Winner.

d) In order to increase the difficulty, start with a joint score of 30; play with 2 dice. One child adds, the other subtracts the total of both dice. The winner is the one who reaches 60 (if adding) or 0 (if subtracting).

Mixed bags: The child is to use the digits and symbols in the mixed bag to make a true statement.

Two children compete.
A card with a number bond is turned over.
One child works it out on a calculator.
The other child works it out mentally.
The Winner has the card.

29

Number patterns

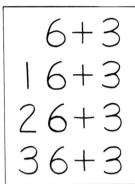

6 + 3
16 + 3
26 + 3
36 + 3

Addition work which emphasises the pattern of number. This could be done by using a number line. Similar patterns can be built up by subtraction.

4, 14, ☐, 34, 44, ☐.

5, 10, 15, 20, ☐, 30.

Number series to be completed emphasising the patterns involved.

Place value

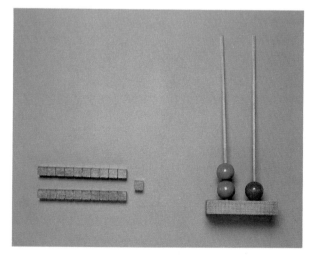

Translation of number values directly from Base 10 apparatus to an abacus.

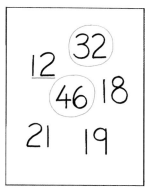

Circle all numbers worth more than 3 tens.
Underline the number that is worth the most
(or least).

Number circles: Two circles are assembled,
face upwards, with a paper fastener through
the centre, the smaller circle on top of the
larger. The child rotates the smaller circle
until the segments match those on the larger
circle. The two numbers in each segment are
then added. *trp* 27, 28

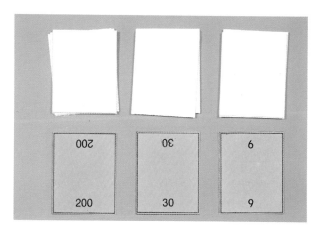

Place value cards: There are three packs of
cards: one of Hundreds, one of Tens, and
one of Units. The child takes one card from
each pack, adds them, and writes the
total. *trp* 29, 30

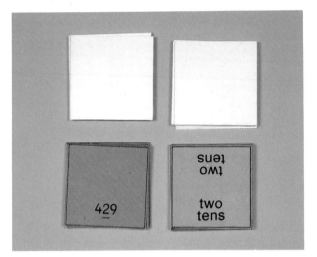

Place value matching game: A card from each pile of number cards and word cards is turned over by each child in turn. When two cards match in value (e.g. the ones illustrated), the child keeps the pair of cards. *trp* 31, 32

Caley addition-grid where one of the sets of figures to be added is an exact number of Tens (or Hundreds). *trp* 2

+	10	20	30	40	50
6					
8			38		
9					
7					
4					

Book I

The following pages detail the content of each page of Peak Book I shown under chapter headings, and where appropriate include comments upon specific teaching points. It also suggests, chapter by chapter, further activities which supplement, consolidate or extend the skills being developed.

Addition

The child should by now be able to add Hundreds, Tens and Units, and have a good understanding of place value. Book I reinforces the skills of place value of Hundreds, Tens and Units, and applies these skills in problem situations.

Addition and Subtraction are treated separately in their own chapters of the book to allow for maximum organisational flexibility. The further activities which follow sometimes include a combination of addition and subtraction skills.

More practice examples can be found on pages 56–58 of the Pupils' Book.

Further activities

Place value   Use prepared duplicated abacus sheets *trp* 3

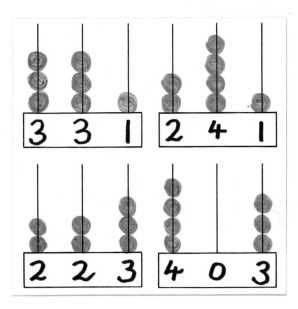

How many different numbers can be shown on a spike abacus using 7 beads?
Record on abacus sheets.
Give the child the opportunity to say the numbers.

Questions which could be asked:
Which is the largest number you have made?
Which is the smallest number you have made?
Can you make this number 10 smaller? (remove a bead from the ten spike).
Can you make this number 100 larger? (add a bead to the hundred spike).
Similar activities can be done with a different number of beads.
The duplicated abacus sheets can also be used for the work on page 7 in the Pupils' Book.

Calculator activities

"Zap the 9"

Game of ZAP: Child A displays a three digit number, then nominates which digit is to be zapped.

The 9 has been changed to 0 by −90.

Child B replaces the nominated digit with a zero by subtracting.

Each digit may be "zapped" in turn.

"Change 2 to 8"

Change the digit: Child A displays a three digit number, then nominates which digit is to be changed.

The 2 has been changed by +60.

Child B changes to the new digit by an addition or subtraction operation.

[The original number may be recorded to save disagreements.]

The children take it in turns to nominate and to change the digits.

Operations

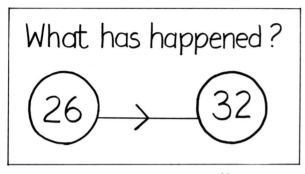

What has happened ?

(Answer +6)

The child has to decide whether it is an addition or subtraction situation.

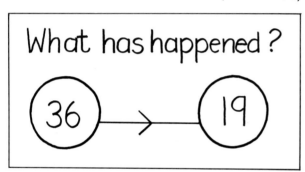

What has happened ?

The numbers used can be varied to make it a number bond activity or a computational exercise.

In the Pupils' Books, the title of each chapter suggests the operation involved. It is sensible, therefore, to provide some activities which require the child to recognise the operation from the language used. In the following activity the numbers used can be small (less than 30) to make it a number bond exercise, or larger to test an understanding of place value. You may wish to use this activity after the child has completed both the addition and subtraction chapters.

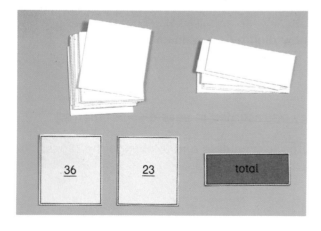

Number operation cards: Prepare squares of card with numbers on, and rectangles of card with the language of operations on. *trp* 33, 34 The cards are arranged in two piles, face down. The child turns over two numbers, and one operation.
He then carries out the appropriate operation. When all the numbers/operations are used up, the packs can be shuffled and re-used.

Length

The child should have gained an understanding of the concept of Length, using arbitrary units, from the work done in the Infant Section of the scheme. He should also be able to choose a suitable arbitrary unit for any given measuring task. It is now an appropriate time to introduce standard units of length. The centimetre is the most convenient standard unit to which the child can be introduced.

Page no.	Content	New language
12	Introduction of cm. Measuring in cm	centimetre cm
13	Measuring and drawing lines in cm	
14	Measuring objects in cm	
15	Estimating and measuring objects in cm	

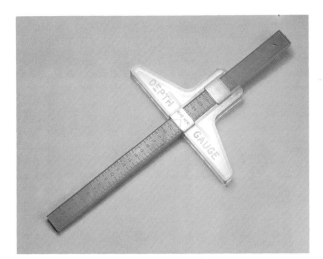

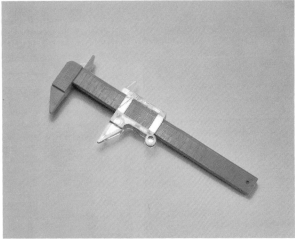

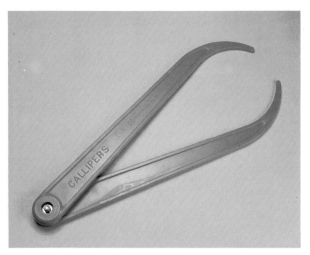

Whilst the child is involved in measuring activities he should be given the opportunity to select a suitable measuring tool for the task in hand.

Through these measuring activities the child will be concerned with:
measuring and recording
measuring to the nearest centimetre
estimation before measurement
It is also important that the child should meet all the relevant
mathematical language during these activities (e.g. wide, thick,
narrow etc.).

Further activities

The concept of "height from the ground" is not dealt with in the
Pupils' Books. It is important to teach, for the purposes of this
concept, that height is measured from the ground to the underside of
the object: the height of an object from the ground does not depend
upon its size.

These three children, although different in size, are at the same
height from the ground.

Worksheet activity

Colour the highest/lowest balloon; apple; climber.

Length strips: Measuring activities can be used to consolidate number language. Prepare various strips of card *trp* 34. Each strip to be an exact number of centimetres. Cards can be prepared asking:

1. Find strips which have a difference of 2 cm.
2. Find strips which have a total length of 13 cm.
3. Find two strips where one is half as long as the other.
4. Find two strips where one is double the length of the other.
5. Put two strips together. Find a strip which is the same length.
6. Put two strips together. Find another two strips which are the same length.

The child answers the problem by an appropriate method, side matching or measuring.

Subtraction

Up to now the child has been involved in subtraction bonds up to 20, and all subtraction has taken place in horizontal form. Four aspects of subtraction were developed in the Infant Section; taking away, counting back, counting on, and difference. The fact that a relationship exists between addition and subtraction bonds was also established, i.e.

$$\text{If} \quad 14 = 6 + 8$$
$$\text{Then} \quad 14 - 6 = 8$$
$$14 - 8 = 6$$

Having developed the concept of place value, we are now able to proceed to the subtraction of larger numbers where decomposition is involved. For a child to gain a sound understanding of the process of subtraction, it is important for him to work systematically through the many stages which are necessary to this understanding.

Page no.	Content	New language
16–17	Subtraction of Tens and Units (no decomposition)	
18–20	Subtraction of Tens and Units (with decomposition)	
21–23	Subtraction problems	

Pages 16–17 This is an introduction to subtraction in a vertical format using structured apparatus. At this stage there will be no decomposition necessary as the child first has to learn the mechanics of subtraction using apparatus on a place value sheet. We suggest that place value sheets be prepared showing the three columns H T U *trp* 17, 18. You will notice on the place value sheets in the Pupils' Books that only the first number in the subtraction is put out, the second number indicates the amount to be taken away.

Use your discretion about when to expect the child to stop using the apparatus.

The child should not proceed to the next stage until he can cope with this stage in the abstract, and you may have to provide more practice examples.

Pages 18–20 This is subtraction of Tens and Units where decomposition is involved. We suggest that subtraction by decomposition is suitable since it can easily be illustrated in concrete form using structured apparatus. When this is done, the problem of children wrongly subtracting the smaller digit from the larger is eliminated.

Before a child subtracts in the abstract, it is necessary to show him how to record. A possible method of recording is shown on page 18 of the Pupils' Book.

On pages 59–61 of the Pupils' Book there are more practice examples if they are required, but children should be able to work proficiently in the abstract.

Further activities

The following activities will help to develop:
  a) the equivalences involved in subtraction
  b) the relationship between addition and subtraction.
Each of these activities, using M.A.B. apparatus, should be developed into workcard/worksheet activities.

You may wish the child to record this activity as a formal subtraction

$$\begin{array}{r} 34 \\ -6 \\ \hline 28 \end{array}$$

6 was taken away

The relationship between addition and subtraction can be further developed.

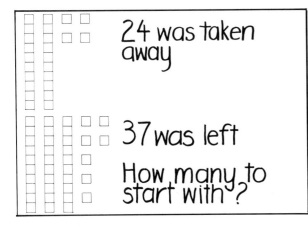

Although this is a "subtraction" problem, to obtain the answer an addition must take place.
The child can record this as a formal subtraction:

$$\begin{array}{r} 61 \\ -24 \\ \hline 37 \end{array}$$

61 to start with

The child should recognise that a subtraction has occurred. The recording may be:

$$\begin{array}{r} 23 \\ -9 \\ \hline 14 \end{array}$$

9 was subtracted

The child should recognise that an addition has occurred. To discover the missing number a subtraction is necessary
The recording may be:

$$\begin{array}{r} 23 \\ + 8 \\ \hline 31 \end{array}$$

8 was added

The Frame Abacus is an excellent piece of apparatus for developing and extending number bonds and for quick methods. It can also be used to consolidate the equivalences involved in T U

Show 23 on one side.
Subtract 9.
Discuss the best method of doing this.

Shape

In the earlier work, children were made aware of the natural and geometric shapes, and in particular the simple properties of the plane shapes (square, circle, rectangle and triangle) and the solid shapes (sphere, cube, cuboid and cylinder). In Book I, this work is consolidated and the triangular prism and cone are introduced.

 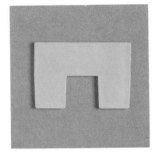

In tessellating activities, children should use shapes which do not tessellate, as well as those which do. Do not restrict the shapes to the usual polygons.

Further activities

Children will have sorted shapes into two groups; those which tessellate and those which do not. Each of these two groups may be investigated further.

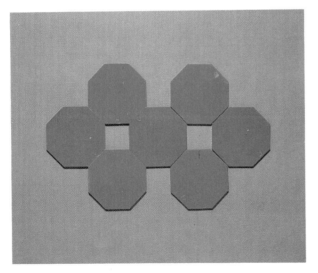

Choose a non-tessellating shape.
Can you arrange the shape to leave a regular "gap"? e.g. an octagon can be arranged to leave "gaps" of triangles or squares.

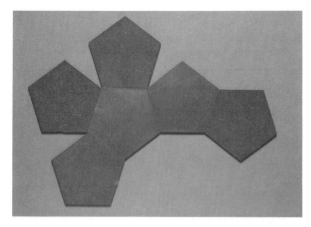

Repeat for other shapes.

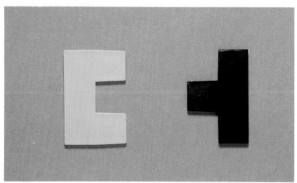

Children can tessellate with more than one shape at a time.

A collection of rubbings can be made of tessellating shapes in the environment.

brick wall

man-hole cover

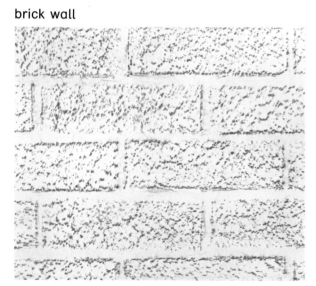

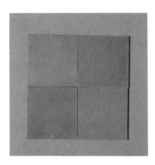

Take a square.
Can you tessellate it to make a larger square?

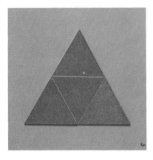

Take a triangle.
Can you tessellate it to make a larger triangle?

Repeat this for other shapes.

Tessellations can be used as an introduction to work on area. The shapes chosen can be used as arbitrary units for finding area. In the following activities it is important to remember:
1. The child should be given the opportunity to estimate.
2. Discussion is vital as to the degree of accuracy you want, i.e. what to do with the bits of shapes at the edges.
3. The activities should aim to develop, for the child, an ability to select an appropriate unit with which to measure.

How many rectangles cover your book?
How many triangles cover your book?
What other shape can you use to measure it with?

Draw round your shoe.
How many squares cover it?
How many hexagons cover it?
What other shape can you use to measure it with?

Multiplication

In the Infant Section the child had experience in repeated addition by counting, and early ideas of commutativity using structured apparatus were developed. This chapter gives further experience of repeated addition in number pattern form.

Page no.	Content	New language
28	Repeated addition of 2, up to 20	
29	Repeated addition of 5, up to 50	
	Repeated addition of 10, up to 100	

Further activities

Ample opportunity should be given of building up number patterns of 2, 5, 10. Prepare various *number squares*, trp **4.**

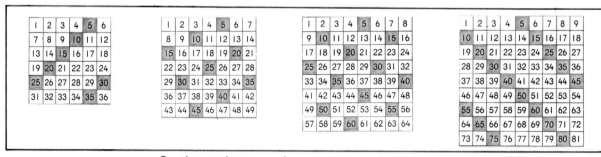

On the various number squares colour each multiple of 5.
What patterns do you get?
Repeat this for patterns of 2 and 10.

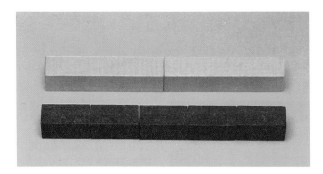

Number rods (Cuisenaire, Colour Factor, Stern) were suggested for demonstrating early ideas of commutativity in Infant Handbook 2 page 85. This should be developed further.

How many 2 rods match the two 5 rods?

Prepare some card rectangles. (If you are using Cuisenaire the sides must be an exact number of cm, if you are using Stern the sides must be in units of 19 mm/¾ in.)

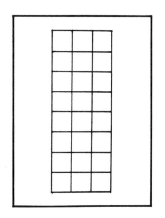

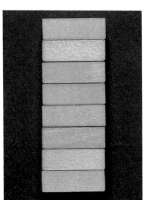

Will the 6 rods exactly cover the 24 rectangle?
Will the 5 rods exactly cover the 24 rectangle?
Change the rectangle and repeat. This activity leads into early ideas of factors.

Capacity

In the earlier work in the Infant Section, the child gained experience in measuring using arbitrary units. It is now an appropriate time to introduce standard units, and the unit introduced in this chapter is the litre.

Page no.	Content	New language
30–31	Use of litre measure to fill other containers	litre l estimate

In these measuring activities we suggest that the child measures to the nearest litre. This is developing the idea of approximation as was previously done with arbitrary units. The child records estimates before actually measuring, and when his estimates become reasonably accurate, it is an indication that he has an appreciation of the units involved.

Further activities

Have a collection of litre containers to give a visual appreciation of what I litre looks like. The containers could be filled with coloured water.

Use various containers to fill I litre e.g. egg-cups, tins, beakers.

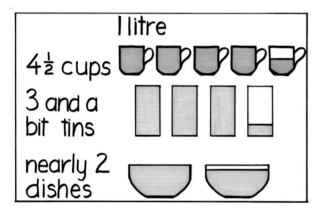

The results could be displayed pictorially.

Fractions

Although $\frac{1}{4}$ and $\frac{1}{2}$ may well have arisen incidentally in the Infant Section, no attempt has been made up to this point to establish any equivalence between various fractions. In this chapter, $\frac{1}{4}$ and $\frac{1}{2}$ are introduced and the equivalences between them and a whole one.

Page no.	Content	New language
32–33	Introduction of $\frac{1}{2}$ by paper folding; equivalence with a whole one	half $\frac{1}{2}$
34	Halving shapes by lines	
35	Introduction of $\frac{1}{4}$ by paper folding; equivalence with a whole one	quarter $\frac{1}{4}$

Although this chapter introduces the $\frac{1}{4}$, and its equivalence with a whole one, it does not deal with the equivalence between $\frac{1}{4}$, $\frac{1}{2}$ and $\frac{3}{4}$. This is dealt with at a later stage.

Further activities

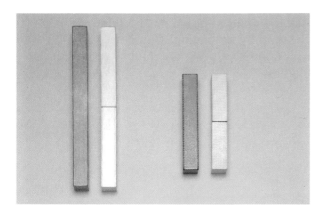

Use number rods for comparison to show two halves make a whole.
Discuss with the child which rods cannot be used in this way (i.e. the odd numbers).

These are halves of shapes.
What do the whole shapes look like?
The shapes could be templates for the children to draw round or they could be on worksheets for the children to fold and cut out.
For some of the shapes various solutions are possible.

Have two identical containers. (Bottoms of plastic lemonade bottles.)
Partially fill one container.
Ask child to pour half into the other container.
Final result is checked by side matching the containers. Much discussion is needed.

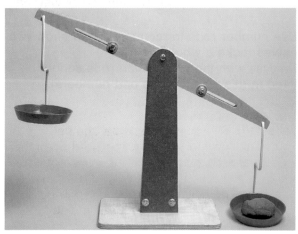

Put a lump of plasticine on some scales. Ask the child to halve it. The final result is checked by balancing. Could be repeated with sand/rice/peas etc. Much discussion is needed.

Weight

In the earlier work in the Infant Section, the child gained experience in weighing items using arbitrary units. It is now an appropriate time to introduce standard units, and the unit introduced in this chapter is the gram. The activities involve the child in balancing items against a given weight. We do not advise using single grams as they are impracticable at this stage.

Page no.	Content	New language
36	Introduction of gram weights, and g	grams g
37	Weighing of commodities in grams	

Further activities

How many 20 g weights balance 100 g?

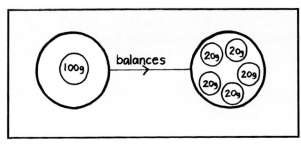

Recording can be done in this form.
Similar activities possible with other weights.

Allow the child ample opportunity of balancing objects against various weights. In the balancing activities ensure the child adds the weights to the pan in a logical orderly manner e.g. he does not add a 20 g weight, then a 50 g weight, then another 20 g weight. He must realise that he needs to start with the largest weight which is lighter than the object, and then add a progression of smaller weights.

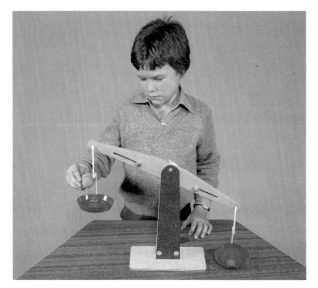

Weigh 50 g of plasticine.
Make two 25 g weights from the plasticine.

Give the child a 50 g weight, a 20 g weight and plasticine.
Can the child make a 30 g weight from plasticine?

Division

Early ideas of division were introduced in the Infant Section with the child dividing objects into equal groups, and later into a given number of groups. This chapter extends this experience with practical sharing into groups, using structured apparatus. There is no decomposition involved at this stage.

The sharing is restricted to Tens and Units with no decomposition T → U involved. It is vital that when the child shares using the apparatus that he shares the Tens first, then the Units, even though no decomposition is involved. This is a preparation for formal computation.

Further activities

Using number rods, decompose a number into equal sub-sets. Repeat for various numbers.

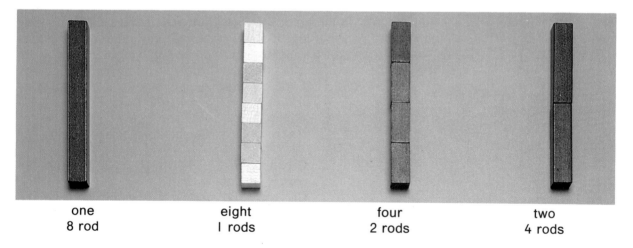

one	eight	four	two
8 rod	1 rods	2 rods	4 rods

Money

The child has had experience of coin recognition and the equivalences involved, and simple addition and subtraction problems in practical situations involving coins. In this chapter the work is consolidated with further addition and subtraction problems of a practical nature involving amounts up to £1.

Further activities

Prepare *domino cards* trp 35, 36 to give practice in equivalence of coins. If the cards are to be made, use either rubber stamp of coins or stick-on replicas.

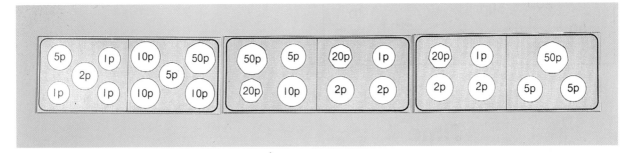

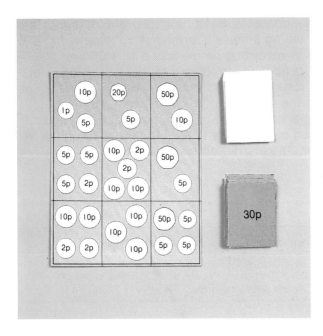

Prepare *Money Matching cards* trp 37, 38 showing various groups of coins in each square. For each board, have a matching pack of cards showing various single total amounts. Each child has to match his 9 squares with the amount shown on his lotto board. The child who does it the quickest is the Winner.

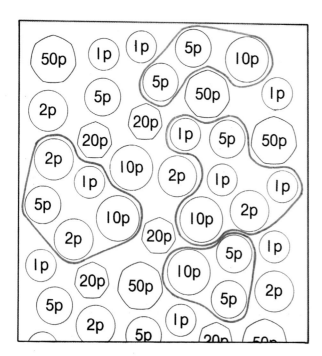

Prepare duplicated sheets showing various coins *trp* 5.
Make sets of 20p.
Repeat for other totals on identical sheets.

Time

There are three main concepts in teaching time:
    1. The concept of time—appreciation of how long a minute etc. is.
    2. The oral method of telling time—"quarter past"; "twenty to" etc.
    3. The written method of recording time—3.20 p m; 4.05 a m; 2330.
In the Infant Section, the child was introduced to the oral notation of telling the time, and this form of telling the time, whether at school or in the home, is based on the "o'clock", "minutes past", "minutes to" notation. However, the alternative form of notation (e.g. 40 minutes past 6) is the main method of *recording* time, and this is carefully developed in this chapter. The shortened form (e.g. 6.10, 8.50) is introduced in *Book 3*.

Further activities

Using a sand timer or Osmiroid tocker:
How many words can you read?
How many sums can you do?
How many skips? etc.

Graphs

Earlier work introduced the child to the idea of pictorial representation in a simple form, and the interpretation of these picture graphs. This chapter develops the idea of a picture graph into column graphs. At this stage only a scale of I : I is involved.

Page no.	Content	New language
48–49	Interpretation of picture graphs	
50–51	Drawing of column graphs (scale I : I)	column graphs

It may be sensible to introduce the idea of a column graph initially as a class, or large group, activity. Take care to structure the information to be graphed, so that one square on the graph paper represents one person or one item.

Emphasis should be laid on the correct placing of labels on the graph, particularly on the two axes; the vertical axis requires labels on lines, the horizontal axis requires them in spaces for column graphs.

Further activities

Care should be taken to ensure that any subject matter used for drawing column graphs will give numbers to be graphed which do not require the use of a scale. For this reason, children cannot at this stage be allowed to collect information in a random way: the activity needs teacher guidance.

Suitable subjects for graphing are:
Bedtimes.
Amount of pocket money (do not overlap; i.e. amounts should perhaps be 0–19p, 20–39p, 40–59p, etc).
Favourite food.

Investigations

In all pupils' materials from now on, there will be an Investigations chapter. Most of the situations presented will be of an open-ended nature and will not necessarily result in one particular solution for a given problem. The number of solutions and the time spent on each problem are discretionary.

Page no.	Content	New language
52	Investigation of shapes, using a 9 pin geoboard	geoboard spotty paper
53	Properties of number using structured apparatus	

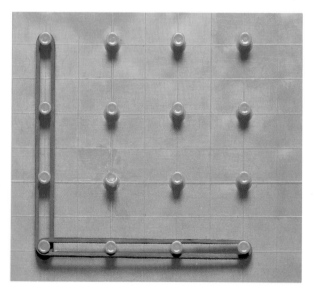

A large geoboard can be reduced by blanking off pins with elastic bands.

This is a 16 pin board blanked off to create a 9 pin board.

Discussion is necessary with the child to ensure what is meant by "different". It would be sensible to define "different" as different in shape and/or size.

A suitable way of recording geoboard work is on square lattice paper, sometimes called *spotty paper*, *trp* 6, 7, 8.

Further activities

a) Geoboard activities (page 52)
   Each of the activities can be extended to a 16 pin geoboard.

b) Properties of number (page 53)
   The activity using number rods could be extended:

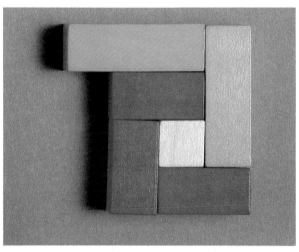

Continue this pattern.
How many 4 rods will be needed?
How many 5 rods?

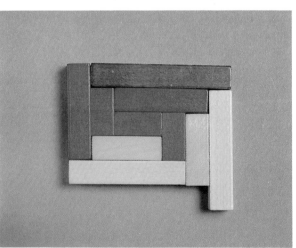

Begin with a 2 rod in the middle.
How many 4 rods?
How many 5 rods?

Problem pages

These pages allow the child to apply the numerical skills, acquired earlier, in a problem situation.

Page no.	Content	New language
54–55	Simple number problems	

More practice

The "more practice" pages are included for those children for whom the teacher feels extra practice in computational skills is desirable. It may well be that for many children the work on these pages will not be necessary.

    The "more practice" pages can also be used, of course, for revision purposes.

Page no.	Content	New language
56–58	More practice—addition of Hundreds, Tens and Units	
59–61	More practice—subtraction of Tens and Units	

Assessment (pages 62–63)

The major teaching points are tested in these assessment pages, and they must be completed before going on to the next stage. If mistakes arise in the test, care should be taken that they are not due to a lack of understanding of the concepts and skills involved.

Book 2

The following pages detail the content of each page of Peak Book 2, shown under chapter headings and where appropriate, include comments upon specific teaching points. They also suggest, chapter by chapter, further activities which supplement, consolidate or extend the skills being developed.

Addition

The child has had experience in the addition of Hundreds, Tens and Units (with conversion U → T → H) with application to problem situations. This chapter introduces the Thousand, and extends the child's skills to include addition of Thousands, Hundreds, Tens and Units.

Page no.	Content	New language
4	Simple addition bonds (mental work)	
5	Addition of Hundreds, Tens and Units	
6	Introduction of a Thousand; equivalence of Thousands and Hundreds	Thousand
7	Abacus work, involving Thousands	
8–9	Addition of Thousands, Hundreds, Tens and Units	

The introduction of thousands should cause few problems providing the child has a sound understanding of earlier place value work. The use of Base 10 structured apparatus in introducing thousands is highly desirable. If further practice in the addition of Thousands, Hundreds, Tens and Units is necessary, turn to page 64 of the Pupils' Book, which contains further practice examples.

Further activities

A game for 2 children.

front of card   back of card

Make a pack of cards with numbers (in figures) on the front. Underline one digit.
On the back of the card write the value (in words) of that digit.
Each child in turn states the value of the underlined digit.

If he is correct he keeps the card.
The child with the greater number of cards at the end is the Winner.

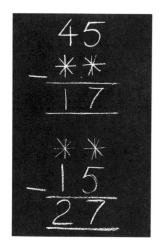

Filling in missing figures where the operation required could be either addition or subtraction.

Even though the sign suggests it is a subtraction operation, it may be necessary to add in order to find the solution.

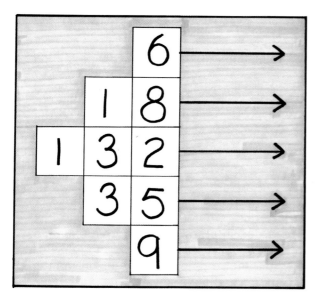

The child is to make up the questions:

a) using addition only
b) using addition and subtraction
c) using addition and multiplication

Calculator work

Ask the child to show a 3 digit number on the calculator (e.g. 236), and record it. Write a new 3 digit number (e.g. 436). Change the number showing on the calculator to the new one in one operation. Similar activities can be used to test place value, but using a subtraction situation (e.g. change 493 to 393).

| 7 | +7 → | 14 | +7 → | 21 | +7 → | 28 | +4 → | 32 | +4 → | 36 |

The child can use only two digits (e.g. 7, 4), and the signs + − =.
Find the fewest number of steps to reach 36.

(A method of recording is shown above.)

Prepare a pack of addition and subtraction cards, each with a bond which could be done mentally (e.g. 28 + 9, 26 − 17).
One child attempts to do each one mentally, whilst a partner works them out on a calculator.
Whoever finds the answer first wins the card.

Length

The child has met the standard unit of a centimetre and has estimated, measured and recorded in practical measuring situations. This chapter involves computation using a centimetre, and in a practical situation introduces the metre as a unit of measurement and the equivalences between a metre and centimetres. The work leads to addition in metre notation.

Page no.	Content	New language
10	Measuring in cm	
11	Addition in cm	
12	Introduction of metre; m	metre m
13	Measuring in m, cm	
14	Introduction of metre notation	
15	Addition of length (metre notation)	

Pages 14–15 These pages introduce addition in metre notation and involve the use of a decimal point. At this stage the decimal point is simply a separator between metres and centimetres and no attempt should be made to explain its function as a true decimal. This will be done in later books.

If the child needs further practice in addition in metre notation, turn to page 69 of the Pupils' Book.

Further activities

Give the child plenty of experience of measuring around circular objects, such as hoops, balls etc. Establish the idea of "rolling" the objects in order to measure the distance around them. This idea can then be transferred to the trundle wheel, so that it can be used as a measuring tool.

Children need experience of estimating and measuring longer distances (in metres).
From a point in the playground, estimate the distances of various objects.
Use the trundle wheel to measure the actual distances (to the nearest metre).

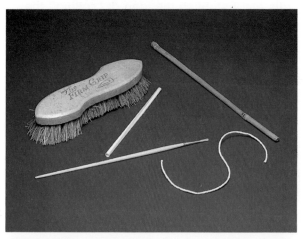

Collect a small number of items of different lengths, e.g. from 50 cm to 1·50 m.
Structure your questions to suit the objects:
Which objects have a difference in length of 2 or 3 cm?
Which object is half the length of the cane?
Which two objects have a total length of 2·45 m? etc.

Encourage measurement and recording in metre notation.

Measure objects such as the centre of a kitchen roll with calipers, diameter measure, depth gauge.

Graph heights of children/family. The wall could represent the first metre, with the people showing an appropriate height above the wall.

Subtraction

Subtraction involving decomposition from Tens and Units has already been introduced, and this chapter extends the child's skills to include decomposition from Hundreds to Tens, and from Hundreds to Tens to Units. The language of subtraction and its application to problem situations is reinforced.

Page no.	Content	New language
16	Simple subtraction activities	
17	Subtraction of Hundreds, Tens and Units (with decomposition T → U)	
18	Subtraction of Hundreds, Tens and Units (with decomposition H → T)	
19	Subtraction of Hundreds, Tens and Units (with decomposition T → U, H → T)	
20–21	Subtraction of Hundreds, Tens and Units (with decomposition H → T → U)	
22–23	Language of subtraction	
24	Subtraction problems	

Pages 17–21   The extension of decomposition to Hundreds, Tens and Units is very carefully graded in this chapter. Each new situation is introduced in a practical way, with appropriate examples to follow, so that by the end of the chapter, the example requiring decomposition from the Hundreds column right across to the Units column can be handled.

Again you can use your discretion as to when you can expect the child to work in the abstract without resorting to the apparatus.

Although the Pupils' Book only shows a place value sheet with H T U columns, sheets showing the four columns (Th H T U) can be used.

Pages 20–21   You will notice that the Tens column in each example has "0" on the top line which will involve a decomposition from H → T → U.

If the child needs further practice in the subtraction of Hundreds, Tens and Units, you can turn to pages 65 and 66 of the Pupils' Book.

Further activities

"*Crossnumber*" puzzles are a useful means of revising the language of formal operations, *trp* 9. They can be written to concentrate on one operation, or include all number operations.

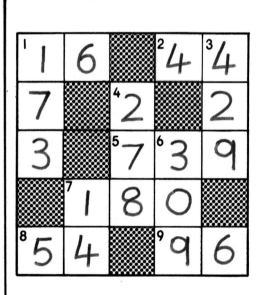

Across

1. 14 less than 30
2. Subtract 56 from 100
5. From 800 take 61
7. 256 minus 76
8. The difference between 104 and 50
9. Take 4 from 100

Down

1. 200 is 27 greater than this number
3. 71 from 500 leaves this number
4. From 628 subtract 350
6. Add this number to 100 to make 409
7. The difference between 86 and 100

Calculator game for two.

First child enters any number between 50 and 100. His partner has to reduce the number to 50 by one subtraction operation on the calculator.

Shape

The child is now familiar with four plane shapes (square, circle, rectangle and triangle) and six solid shapes (cube, cuboid, cylinder, sphere, cone and triangular prism). This chapter explores the properties of faces, edges and vertices of the known solid shapes, and introduces the hexagon.

Page no.	Content	New language
24–25	Introduction of faces, edges and vertices	face, edge, vertex, vertices
26	Counting of faces on solid shapes	
27	Introduction of the hexagon	hexagon

The term "face" has been restricted to flat surfaces and the term "edge" to straight edges. You could include other solid shapes which have curved faces and curved edges if you wish to do so.

Further activities

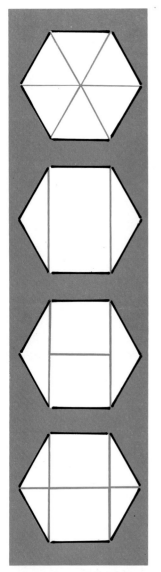

Cutting up regular hexagons *trp* 43:
Cut up a hexagon to make 6 triangles.

Cut up a hexagon to make 2 equal triangles and a rectangle.

Cut up a hexagon to make 2 equal triangles and 2 equal rectangles.

Cut up a hexagon to make 4 equal triangles and 2 equal rectangles.

Make hexagons on a 16 pin geoboard.
This activity will allow children to form non-regular hexagons.
Results may be copied on to *spotty paper*, *trp* 7.

Use *hexagon-covered mathematical paper*, trp II.
Child draws a pattern on 7 hexagons as shown below. He then cuts out the 7 hexagons. Partner has to remake the original pattern.

Angles

This chapter introduces the child to the idea of turn—direction of turn and amounts of turn.

Page no.	Content	New language
28	Direction of turn, introducing clockwise and anti-clockwise	clockwise anti-clockwise
29	Introduction of amounts of turn—$\frac{1}{4}$ turn, $\frac{1}{2}$ turn, full turn	

Further activities

Ask child to find out whether things in school turn clockwise or anti-clockwise. Use things which are familiar e.g. taps, door knobs, keys, etc.

What happens when the tap is turned anti-clockwise?
Which way does the door knob turn to open the door?
Which way does the key turn to wind up the clock?
Which way does the door turn to open?

Spinner game trp 39. Children have spinner, divided into segments. Spinner indicates number of moves, and whether clockwise or anti-clockwise.
Child puts counter on "Start" and spins the spinner, moving the counter the number of spaces shown in the direction indicated.
The Winner is the child who lands exactly on "Finish".

Multiplication

The idea of repeated addition has already been introduced in number pattern form. This chapter includes the formal build up of the tables 2, 3, 4, 5, 6 and 10. It is important that the tables covered are committed to memory.

Page no.	Content	New language
30–31	Building up of ×2 and 2× tables	
32	Building up of ×5 and 5× tables, ×10 and 10× tables	
33	Practice in simple multiplication facts	
34	Multiplication of Tens and Units by 2, 5	
35	Building up of 3, 4, 6 tables Multiplication by 2, 3, 4, 5, 6, 10	

The practical build up of tables is to illustrate to the child that multiplication is repeated addition and eventually that $2 \times 3 = 3 \times 2$ (i.e. the commutative law, early ideas of which were introduced in the Infant Section). You will notice that in each case the number shown first in the multiplication situation is the number in the group, and the second number indicates the operation (i.e. 2×3 is 2 counters set out 3 times).

It is important that the tables written in the child's book are checked.

Further practice in formal multiplication can be found on page 67 of the Pupils' Book.

Further activities

Simple number searcher:

The answers lie in 2 directions
    → or ←
The child has to ring the answers to these table bonds.
6×3, 4×5, 7×6, 3×5,
8×4, 9×5, 6×6, 4×6

Calculator game, for two children:

One child enters a number less than 50.

The other child has to add on a number, so it becomes a multiple of 4. input + l

First child divides by 4 on the calculator to see if his partner is right. input ÷ 4

The game can be varied (and made more difficult) by adding further rules:
    a) The number to be added must be more than 9.
    b) A number to be subtracted must be more than 9 etc.
    c) The final number must be a multiple of 3 and 4.

The game of beating the calculator, explained in the further activities to Addition on page 62 could also be used for multiplication and division facts.

Digits you can use
2, 4, 6, 8
Signs you can use
× × +
Make the biggest answer possible

An investigation for the more able child.
The child has four digits e.g. 2, 4, 6, 8.
He has two × signs and one + sign.
He must make the biggest answer possible.
If he has two × signs, and one ÷ sign, what is the biggest answer possible?
A calculator could be used if you wish.

22	17	2	54	19	33	38	13	2	9	57	66	29	26	14	17	41
19	8	40	16	33	20	64	48	6	12	56	16	42	60	51	44	29
1	20	38	28	17	40	21	17	34	32	46	52	59	8	17	24	18
31	48	24	64	29	4	24	32	13	8	4	32	9	16	4	14	58
62	24	66	50	22	12	34	19	9	40	5	36	13	28	17	64	26
9	32	14	37	41	36	28	16	15	48	61	20	1	40	2	12	19
41	17	57	14	26	29	66	41	57	9	2	38	33	19	54	17	22

The child has to colour each square that contains a multiple of 4.

The coloured squares will reveal a word. This activity can be extended to other multiples.

Capacity

The child has met the standard unit of a litre and has estimated, measured and recorded in practical measuring situations. This chapter introduces the $\frac{1}{2}$ and $\frac{1}{4}$ litre and the equivalences between them and the litre.

Page no.	Content	New language
36	Filling of litre, $\frac{1}{2}$ litre, $\frac{1}{4}$ litre jugs	
37	Equivalence between litre, $\frac{1}{2}$ litre, $\frac{1}{4}$ litre	

The beaker used in these activities must be smaller than $\frac{1}{4}$ litre.

Further activities

Gather a range of containers for children to work with.
  a) Child puts them in order, largest to smallest.
  b) Group them into roughly $\frac{1}{4}$ l, $\frac{1}{2}$ l and litre containers.
  c) Give child the opportunity to estimate and compare capacities of containers which hold roughly (or exactly) the same amount, but which are very different in shape.

Fractions

Fractions $\frac{1}{2}$ and $\frac{1}{4}$ have been introduced and the relationships with the whole one. This chapter introduces $\frac{3}{4}$, and develops all the equivalences involved.

Page no.	Content	New language
38	Introduction of $\frac{3}{4}$	Three-quarters $\frac{3}{4}$
39	Equivalence of $\frac{1}{2}$ and $\frac{1}{4}$ to whole one	
40–41	Recognition of fractions of shapes—$\frac{1}{4}$, $\frac{1}{2}$, $\frac{3}{4}$	
42	Colouring of fractions of shapes—$\frac{1}{4}$, $\frac{1}{2}$, $\frac{3}{4}$	
43	Equivalence of $\frac{1}{2}$ and $\frac{1}{4}$	
	Addition of $\frac{1}{2}$ and $\frac{1}{4}$, practically	

The concept of fractions is a difficult one for many children, and it is necessary to make sure that a child understands the concept of $\frac{1}{4}$ before proceeding to $\frac{3}{4}$. This understanding is tested when the child is asked to colour $\frac{1}{4}$ of a shape when there are more than four parts in the whole one.

If a child colours only one part then there is some lack of understanding.

Further activities

These activities offer a child the practical experience of finding halves of quantities.

Cover this rod with 2 equal rods.
(Initial rod must be even.)

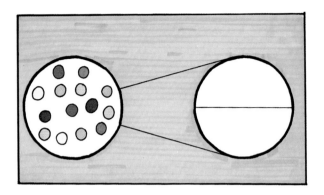

Halving of groups of counters or units.
The reverse operation could also be done i.e. giving a quantity which is a half, and making the full quantity.

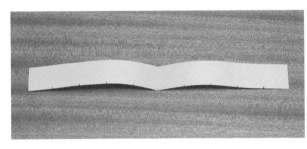

Use paper strips of an exact number of cm.
Child measures strip.
Fold strip in half.
Measure the length of each half.

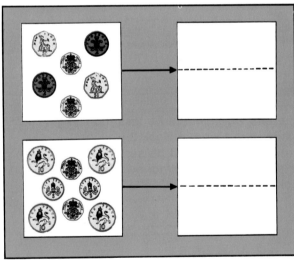

Divide each set of coins into halves (in value).

Early practical work can be done on the techniques of halving quantities of water, plasticine, sand etc., although this needs a great deal of discussion and is perhaps best done by the teacher with a group of children.

A great deal of work can also be done on paper-folding activities to form $\frac{1}{4}$, $\frac{1}{2}$, $\frac{3}{4}$ of original shapes. Similarly, work can be done on the completion of shapes when only $\frac{1}{4}$, $\frac{1}{2}$, or $\frac{3}{4}$ of the shape is shown (suitable for more able children).

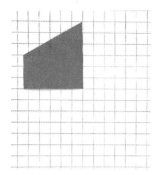

This is a quarter of a shape.
What does the whole shape look like?

Weight

The child has met the standard unit of a gram, and in earlier work was involved in activities where items were balanced against a given weight. This chapter gives the child further opportunities to estimate, weigh and record various objects. The weighing will involve a combination of weights and may involve a degree of approximation. This work leads to addition of weights (in g).

Page no.	Content	New language
44	Practical weighing experience (in g)	
45	Addition of weights (in g)	

The items to be weighed in this work should be less than I kg. (The use of the kilogram weight is introduced in Book 3.)

The work on the addition of grams should be set out formally by the child. There is further practice in the formal addition of weight on page 69 of the Pupils' Book.

Further activities

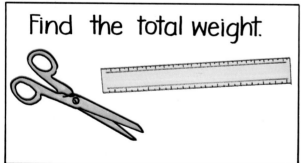

Find the total weight.

Workcards involving the weighing (and addition of weights) of familiar objects in the classroom.

Find the total weight.

Ensure that no combined weights exceed
I kg.

Make 5 small parcels of same size but different weights.
Ask child to put them in order by feeling them, and then weigh them.
Record weights.
Give child work on totalling and differences of weights.
Similar activities could be done with a group of books.

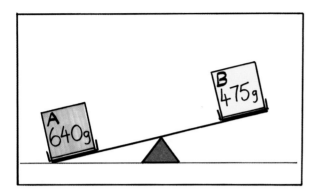

What must be added to parcel B to make the balance level?

Division

The child has had experience of practical sharing using structured apparatus. This experience is extended in this chapter to include decomposition.

Page no.	Content	New language
46	Practical sharing by 2, 3, 4 (no decomposition)	
47	Practical sharing by 2, 3, 4, 5 (with decomposition)	

It is vital that when a child uses structured apparatus for sharing activities in Tens and Units he shares the Tens first, and then the Units.

One should consider very carefully the "patter" used when introducing formal division to children. "Threes into ..." or "How many threes in ..." are typical questions posed to children. Up to this time much work will have been done by children on "sharing" and "dividing into groups". Before using the patter described make sure the child has had experience in dividing quantities into "groups of ...".

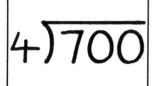

This example stands for both aspects of division and the relevant "patter" indicates which aspect is involved:
  a) How many fours in seven (hundred)?
     (i.e. sharing into groups of 4)
  b) Seven (hundred) divided by 4.
     (i.e. sharing into 4 groups)

Further activities

Using rod apparatus. Early ideas on factors can be developed by using rod apparatus. The following are typical activities:

Put out a 10-rod and 5-rod to make 15
How many 3-rods will match 15?
How many 5-rods will match 15?

How many 2-rods will match 14?
Say how many 7-rods. Were you right?

How many 3-rods will match 12?
Which other rods will match 12?
How many different rods will match 12?

84
8 + 4 = 12
84 ÷ 2 = 42
4 + 2 = 6

Adding digits. Write any 2 digit number where both digits are even.
Add the digits.
Divide the number by 2.
Add the digits.
What do you notice about the addition of the digits (the first answer is double the second one).
Will this always work?
(The digit 0 may be used.)

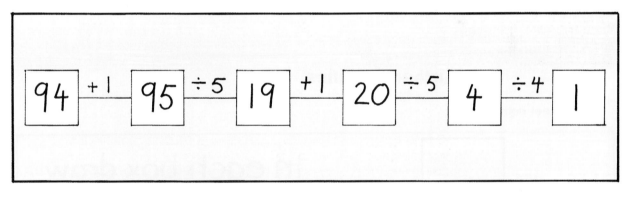

Calculator game: Enter any number between 50 and 100 on calculator. The child can only divide or add, with numbers up to 5. He has to reach 1 in the fewest number of operations. Recording can be done as shown. (If a child, when dividing, gets a decimal answer, he must start again.)
The game is made more difficult by restricting the numbers used to add and divide.

Money

All the coins and the equivalences between them have already been introduced, and the child has met simple addition and subtraction problems in practical situations. This chapter introduces the £ notation, and addition and subtraction using this notation.

This chapter introduces addition and subtraction in £ notation and involves the use of the decimal point. At this stage the decimal point is simply a separator between pounds and pence and no attempt should be made to explain its function as a true decimal. This will be done in later books.

If the child needs further practice of addition and subtraction in £ notation, turn to page 68 of the Pupils' Book.

Further activities

Worksheet activities

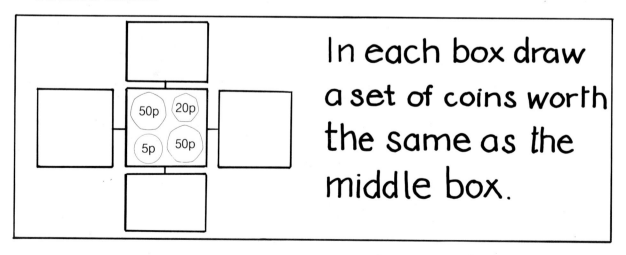

In each box draw a set of coins worth the same as the middle box.

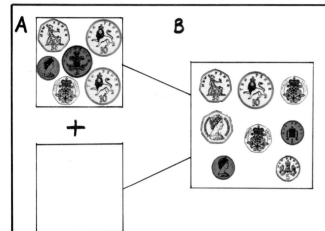

What must be added to set A to make it equal to set B?

What coins can be put into the purse to make a total of £1·50?

How much has been spent if the purse had £2·00 in it?

Pam   Susan   Jane   Wendy.

Who has most money?

Who has least money?

How much have Pam and Jane altogether?

Time

All the early work on Time is built around the "minutes past" notation (e.g. 50 minutes past 1), with its shortened form arising in *Book 3* (e.g. 1.50). We feel that the oral notation for time (e.g. 10 to 2) can be dealt with orally with a class, if you so wish, or left until it arises in *Book 4*.

Page no.	Content	New language
52–53	Simple problems involving minutes past notation	

Children find it difficult to position the hour hand as it moves through the hour. This problem is probably best dealt with by discussion with the children, using a real clock.

Further activities

Any activities which involve the child in the telling of the time, and the recording of it, will be useful. Similarly, activities carried out in a specified period of time (e.g. how many words can you write beginning with "ch" in two minutes).

The recording of time can be woven into story situations. (For *clock faces, trp* 12.)

Draw the times on the clocks from the story.

John set out from home at 10 minutes past 10

to go shopping.

It took him 15 minutes to walk to the shops.

He arrived at the shops at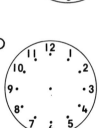

He went to the grocer's.

He left the grocer's shop

at 30 minutes past 10

He arrived home 20 minutes later.

Graphs

The child has met the column graph in a 1 : 1 scale, and the work in this chapter develops the idea of scales.

This chapter introduces the names of the two axes. The information to be graphed is so structured that it enables a scale of 1 : 2 to be used. There is a danger in allowing the child to collect his own information to be graphed at this stage in that it may demand complex scales on the vertical axis.

Again it is important to check the placing of the labels on the graph, particularly on the two axes. The vertical axis requires labels on the lines; the horizontal axis requires them in spaces for column graphs.

Further activities

Other information, suitable for column graphs, which may result in the need for a scale of 1 : 2.

Colour of hair   Size of shoes
Colour of shoes   Size of family
Approximate distance travelled to school.

Investigations

Most of the situations presented in this chapter are of an open-ended nature and do not necessarily result in one particular solution for a given problem. The number of solutions and the time spent on each problem are discretionary.

Further activities

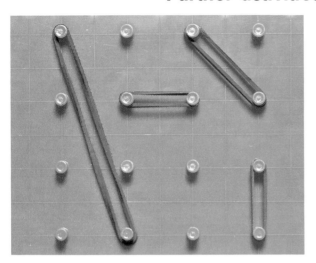

a) Geoboards (pages 58–59)
The geoboard activities can be extended to the use of a 16 pin geoboard.

The 16 pin board offers many more "linkings" of two pins.
The child can be asked to find the longest "link" and the shortest "link".
Recording can be done on spotty paper.

The 16 pin (and 25 pin) boards can be used for similar activities to those on page 59, and other shapes such as the rectangle can be investigated.

b) Number activities (page 60)
This investigation is concerned with the different *ways* of arriving at a number (not the number of different sums). Children should be encouraged to investigate ways of combining operations
(e.g. multiplying 2 numbers and adding a further number: $3 \times 2 + 1$).
With very bright children it could lead on to use of bracket notation, where two operations are used, although this is not formally used in the scheme until much later.

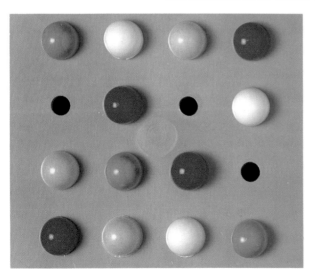

c) Peg board game (page 61)
A simple game on a 4 × 4 peg board, for 4 players. Each player has 4 pegs of one colour. They take turns to put a peg in an empty hole, but no two pegs belonging to one player can be in the same row or column.
If a player cannot put in a peg when it is his turn, he is allowed to move one of his pegs already on the board to a new hole.

The Winner is the one who puts all his pegs in the board first.

Problem pages

These pages allow the child to apply the numerical skills, acquired
earlier, in a problem situation.

Page no.	Content	New language
62–63	Number problems	

More practice

The "more practice" pages are included for those children for whom
the teacher feels extra practice in computational skills is desirable. It
may well be that for many children the work on these pages will not
be necessary.

The "more practice" pages can also be used, of course, for
revision purposes.

Page no.	Content	New language
64	More practice—addition of number	
65–66	More practice—subtraction of number	
67	More practice—multiplication of Tens and Units by 2, 3, 4, 5, 6, 10	
68	More practice—addition and subtraction of money	
69	More practice—addition of m, g	

Assessment (pages 70–71)

The major teaching points are tested in these assessment pages, and
they must be completed before going on to the next stage. If mistakes
arise in the test, care should be taken that they are not due to a lack
of understanding of the concepts and skills involved.

Book 3

The following pages detail the content of each page of Peak Book 3 shown under chapter headings and, where appropriate, include comments upon specific teaching points. It also suggests, chapter by chapter, further activities which supplement, consolidate or extend the skills being developed.

Addition

The child has now acquired the skills of addition and this chapter allows him to practise and apply those skills.

On page 64 of the Pupils' Book there are further practice examples if required.

Further activities

Odd and Even. A game for two children. Each child has 10 counters.
One child is ODD and the other EVEN.
Two (or more) dice are rolled.
If the total is ODD the ODD child claims a counter from his partner, and vice versa.
The child who gains all (or the most) counters is the Winner.

Worksheet activities

63	1	11	13	5	3	9	43	29
87	17	2	10	4	20	8	47	91
55	7	21	23	16	27	31	35	45
7	27	19	23	18	31	33	41	57
33	41	39	47	24	15	29	83	13
29	39	51	55	28	91	97	65	3
73	83	87	81	99	77	73	21	11

Letters and words can be formed on a number grid by colouring odds/evens/multiples etc.
Here the letter T has been formed by colouring all the even numbers.

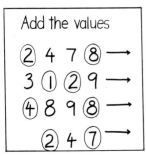

A mental process to test place value.
The values could also be subtracted.

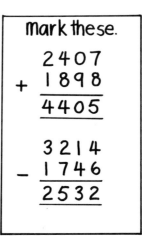

The child marks the problems.

Some of the answers should be incorrect. The subtractions could be checked by addition.

Calculator work

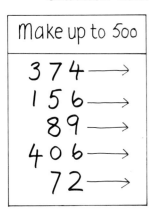

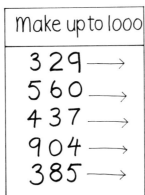

Display the given number.
By one addition make it up to the amount stated.
Results can be recorded as follows:

Input	Operation	Answer
374	+126	500
156	+344	500

Length

The child is familiar with metre notation, and this chapter extends the work to include subtraction in metre notation and introduces measurement of perimeter.

When measuring the perimeter of objects, there may be a degree of approximation required.

On page 69 of the Pupils' Book there is further practice of addition and subtraction of length if required.

Further activities

Workcard activity

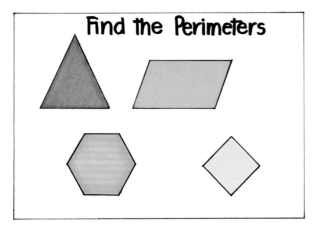

Various shapes are drawn; the sides should be exact cm. Do not restrict the shapes to squares and rectangles.

Group activity

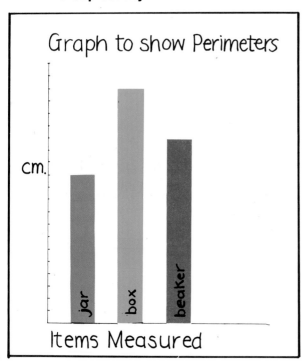

Use long thin strips of paper.
Measure round various items with the strip.
Cut each strip to the perimeter size.
A column graph can be created using these strips.

Cut four identical lengths of string or wool.
Child sticks these lengths on to paper to make
different shapes.
Discussion should show that different shapes
can have the same perimeter.
Areas could be compared if you wish.

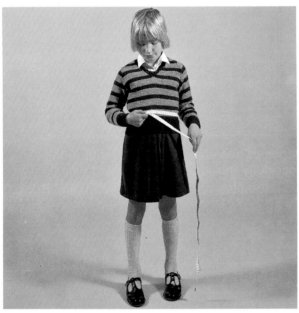

Finding out about yourself.
Is your head as long as your foot?
Is your trunk as long as your leg?
Is your cubit as long as round your waist?
Are you taller than your fathom? (finger tip to
finger tip with arms outstretched).

Calculator work

Enter as metres and add cm.

126
30
252
13
___

The chlid enters the centimetres shown
into the calculator using metre notation.
The answer displayed should be 4.2.1.
This is a self-checking activity involving
metre notation.

Subtraction

Subtraction of Hundreds, Tens and Units has already been developed and this chapter extends the child's skills to include Thousands, Hundreds, Tens and Units. The language of subtraction is reinforced in problem situations.

Page no.	Content	New language
14	Quick subtraction of 9	
15	Subtraction of number and money	
16	Subtraction of Thousands, Hundreds, Tens and Units (including decomposition Th → H)	
17	Subtraction of Thousands, Hundreds, Tens and Units (including decomposition Th → T)	
18–19	Problems	
20	Subtraction of Thousands, Hundreds, Tens and Units (including decomposition Th → U)	
21	Subtraction in words	

As before, the various stages of decomposition dealt with in this chapter have been very carefully introduced in a graded way.

There are more practice examples on page 65 of the Pupils' Book.

Further activities

Number	Digital root	
45	→ 4 + 5 = 9	Write any two digit number.
− 9		Find its digital root.
		Subtract 9
36	→ 3 + 6 = 9	Find the new digital root.
− 9		Repeat this.
27	→ 2 + 7 = 9	What do you notice?
− 9		
etc.		

Worksheet activities   The child should check the given answer by addition.

Mark these.

$$
\begin{array}{r} 5070 \\ -1439 \\ \hline 3521 \end{array}
\qquad
\begin{array}{r} 4201 \\ -\ 972 \\ \hline 3289 \end{array}
\qquad
\begin{array}{r} 2407 \\ -1983 \\ \hline 1424 \end{array}
\qquad
\begin{array}{r} 6091 \\ -2798 \\ \hline 3293 \end{array}
$$

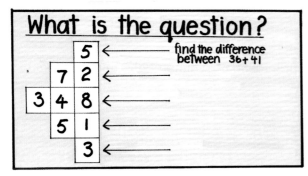

What has happened?

14 ⟶ 36
58 ⟶ 27
42 ⟶ 131
211 ⟶ 96

Record the addition or subtraction which has taken place.

What is the question?

		5	←	find the difference between 36 + 41
	7	2	←	
3	4	8	←	
	5	1	←	
		3	←	

Questions are created by the child which result in the given answers.

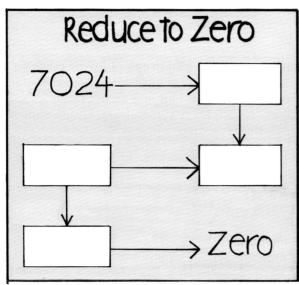

Reduce to Zero

7024 ⟶ ☐

☐ ⟶ ☐

☐ ⟶ Zero

Make 4 subtractions which will eventually give an answer of zero.

Check your subtraction chain with a calculator.

Number	Digital root
462	
	$4 + 6 + 2 = 12 \rightarrow 1 + 2 = 3$
462	
− 99	
363	$3 + 6 + 3 = 12 \rightarrow 1 + 2 = 3$

Write a 3 digit number.
Find its digital root.

Subtract 99.

Find the digital root of the answer.
Does this pattern continue?

571

$$5 + 7 + 1 = 13 \rightarrow 1 + 3 = \mathbf{4}$$

$$\begin{array}{r} 571 \\ - \quad 88 \\ \hline 483 \\ - \quad 88 \\ \hline 395 \end{array}$$

$$4 + 8 + 3 = 15 \rightarrow 1 + 5 = \mathbf{6}$$

$$3 + 9 + 5 = 17 \rightarrow 1 + 7 = \mathbf{8}$$

Write a 3 digit number.
Add its digits.

Subtract 88.
Add the digits of the answer.
Subtract 88.
Add the digits of the answer.
Does this pattern continue?

Shape

This chapter introduces early ideas of symmetry and applies them to natural and plane shapes.

Page no.	Content	New language
22–23	Introduction of line of symmetry	line of symmetry

Further activities

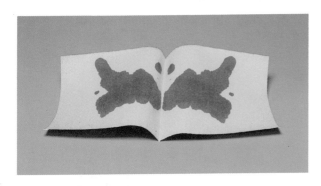

Ink/paint blots: Put drops of ink or paint on a sheet of paper.
Fold the paper in half and smooth out.
Open the paper. A symmetrical shape should have been created.

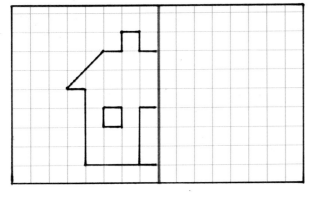

Finish the drawing.
It must be symmetrical.

1	2	3	4	5	6	7	8	9	10
11	12	13	14	15	16	17	18	19	20
21	22	23	24	25	26	27	28	29	30
31	32	33	34	35	36	37	38	39	40
41	42	43	44	45	46	47	48	49	50
51	52	53	54	55	56	57	58	59	60
61	62	63	64	65	66	67	68	69	70
71	72	73	74	75	76	77	78	79	80
81	82	83	84	85	86	87	88	89	90
91	92	93	94	95	96	97	98	99	100

Symmetry in number patterns:
On a *100-square* trp 13 colour the multiples of 2.
How many lines of symmetry can you find?
Repeat for other number patterns.

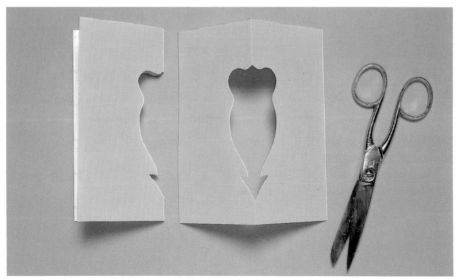

Symmetry in words:
When a mirror is put in the centre of this
word, the word does not change.
Find other words which do not change
i.e. have symmetry.

Fold a sheet of paper
in half.
Cut a piece out of the
folded edge.
Draw what you think
the hole will look like
when you open the
paper.

Were you right?

Book 3

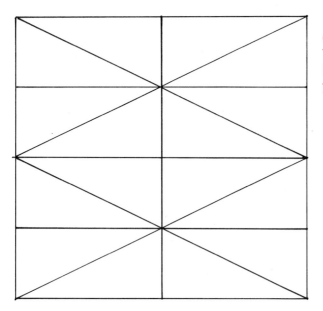

Colour to create a symmetrical pattern.
This could be extended to make your pattern
have only one line of symmetry, or make
your pattern have two lines of symmetry.

Angles

The idea of turn introduced in *Book 2* is now applied to the points of
the compass and right angles.

Children must be shown how to turn the compass so that the
compass needle and the letter N coincide.
    They must be allowed to experiment and discuss what happens
when they turn holding a compass.

Further activities

Children to plan routes around the school using a trundle wheel and the language of direction.

1   Begin at the classroom door 2   Turn right 3   Walk 10 metres 4   Turn left 5   Walk 5 metres   Where are you?

1   Begin at the staffroom 2   Turn North 3   Walk 3 metres 4   Turn East 5   Walk 8 metres 6   Turn South   Where are you?

Left, right, north, south   Face north—what is on your left? right? behind? in front?
Face east—what is on your left? right? behind? in front?
Repeat for other compass points.
Discussion should enable children to realise the difference between "personal direction" (left/right) and compass directions.

Using geostrips

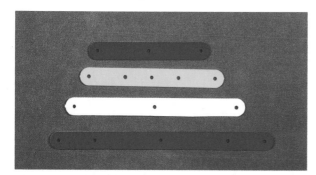

Find strips of different lengths.
Fasten them together to make a shape.
Can you twist your shape to create a right angle?
Rearrange the strips and repeat.

Geoboard activity

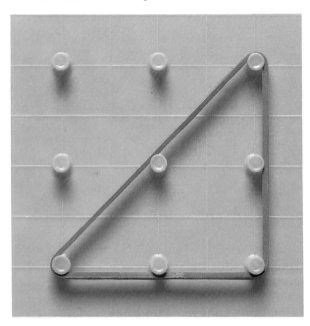

On a 9 pin geoboard make different right
angled triangles.
How many can you make?
Can you make a four-sided shape which has:
    1. only one right angle in it
    2. two right angles in it
    3. three right angles in it
    4. four right angles in it?
Repeat this activity on a 16 pin geoboard.

Take a roughly torn piece of paper. Fold it to make a right-angle.

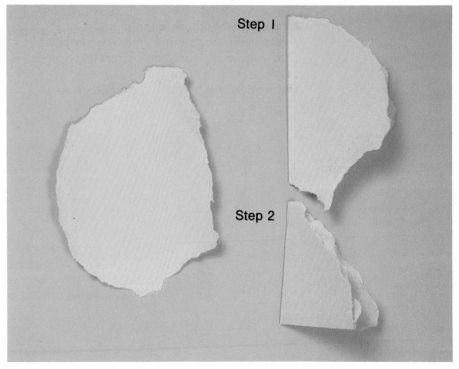

Step 1

Step 2

Multiplication

Earlier work included the build up of all the tables except for 7, 8, 9. This chapter builds up these tables, and gives practice in the skills of multiplication using all the tables.

It is important that the tables written in the child's book are checked, and that all tables covered are committed to memory.

Page no.	Content	New language
28	Multiplication by 2, 3, 4, 5, 6, 10	
29	Build up of 7, 8, 9 tables	
30	Multiplication of Hundreds, Tens and Units by single integers and 10	
31	Problems	

On page 66 of the Pupils' Book there are further practice examples if required.

Further activities

Chance tables

You need two dice.
Throw two dice and multiply their total by four.
Colour in a diamond.
This activity can be changed to suit other multiples.
(For isometric paper, *trp* 14.)

Digital patterns

		End digit
1 × 4 = 4	4
2 × 4 = 8	8
3 × 4 = 12	2
4 × 4 = 16	6
5 × 4 = 20	0
6 × 4 = 24	4
7 × 4 = 28	8
8 × 4 = 32	2
9 × 4 = 36	6
10 × 4 = 40	0

Write the end digit of each multiplication table.
Look at the patterns.
It may be noticed that:
  the 3 times and 7 times patterns are the reverse of each other.
  The 2 times, 4 times, 6 times, and 8 times patterns end in even digits.
  The 9 times pattern decreases by one.

You need two dice.
You can + − × or ÷ the two numbers showing on the dice.
How quickly can you colour in the triangle?

Using digits Choose any three digits (but not 0).
Using each digit once and using the multiplication signs obtain the largest/smallest answer possible.
e.g. using 2, 5, 8

2 × 5 × 8;   25 × 8;   82 × 5;   58 × 2 etc.

Calculator work Using a calculator change from one nominated number to another by multiplying and dividing only.
If a decimal number appears in the display, go back to the beginning.

Change 6 to 400

	× 100	÷ 3	× 2
6	600	200	400

Capacity

The child is familiar with the litre and this chapter introduces him to the millilitre and its equivalences to the litre.

Page no.	Content	New language
32	Introduction of millilitre; ml	millilitre ml
33	Measuring in ml	capacity

It will be necessary to discuss what the marks represent on graduated cylinders and jugs and how to interpret the liquid level at intermediate points.

Equivalence can be demonstrated by careful pouring from the graduated measure into $\frac{1}{4}$, $\frac{1}{2}$ and 1 litre jugs.

Further activities

Pour the same quantity of water into differently shaped plastic bottles. Mark the water level in each. Cut the tops off at this mark to create containers of the same capacity. Use these containers for comparison activities.

Ask the child to check the capacity of various commercial containers. What does the label say the bottle holds? Fill the bottle with water and measure. Is the label correct?

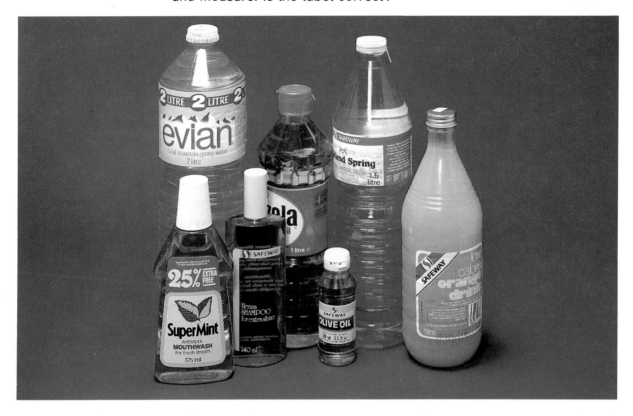

Fractions

The child is familiar with $\frac{1}{4}$, $\frac{1}{2}$, $\frac{3}{4}$, and the equivalences between them. This chapter consolidates this work and introduces $\frac{1}{3}$, $\frac{2}{3}$. It also includes work on finding fractions of quantities.

Page no.	Content	New language
34–35	Recognition of and equivalence between $\frac{1}{4}$, $\frac{1}{2}$, $\frac{3}{4}$, whole one	
36	Introduction of $\frac{1}{3}$, $\frac{2}{3}$	one third $\frac{1}{3}$ two thirds $\frac{2}{3}$
37	Finding $\frac{1}{2}$, $\frac{1}{3}$, $\frac{1}{4}$ of quantities	

Further activities

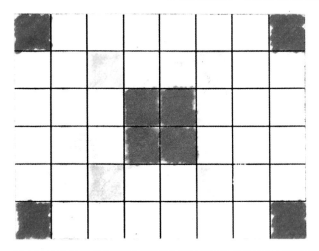

Colour $\frac{1}{4}$ of the squares to make a symmetrical pattern.
Colour $\frac{1}{2}$ of the squares to make a symmetrical pattern.
Now colour $\frac{3}{4}$ of the squares to make a symmetrical pattern.

This is half of a shape. Draw the whole shape

This is quarter of a shape. Draw the whole shape

Experience could be given in halving and quartering during work on other topic areas. The results may be obtained practically or by computation.
Find a half of (or a quarter of):
£1, 1 hour, 1 day, 1 metre, 1 kilogram, 1 litre etc.
The answers should be given in whole units e.g. $\frac{1}{2}$ of £1 = 50p.

Using number rods

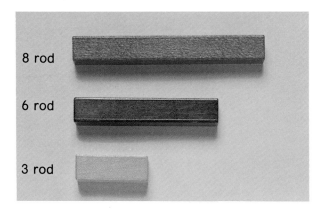

8 rod

6 rod

3 rod

Find $\frac{1}{4}$ of this rod (2 rod)
Find $\frac{3}{4}$ of this rod (6 rod)

This rod is worth half of a number.
This rod is worth $\frac{3}{4}$ of a number.
What are the numbers?

Which rod is $\frac{2}{3}$ of this?

Looking at number

Halve each number.

$4 + 4 + 6 = 14$ What happens to the answer?

$8 \times 2 = 16$ Halve each number.

$36 \div 4 = 9$ What happens to the answer?
Halve one of the numbers.
What happens to the answer?

Activities like this may be extended to quartering, and doubling.

Weight

The computation skills involving grams developed in earlier books are used in a problem situation in this chapter.

Page no.	Content	New language
38–39	Problems involving addition and subtraction of grams	

There are further practice examples involving formal computation on page 69 of the Pupils' Book.

Further activities

Weigh 5 conkers.
Calculate the weight of 20 conkers.
Weigh 20 conkers.
Are your two results the same?
(Discuss the discrepancy with the child.)

Weigh 10 marbles.
Calculate the weight of one marble.
Weigh one marble.
Were you correct?

What is the difference in weight between
10 bolts and 10 screws?
How many bolts are there in 50 g?
How many screws are there in 50 g?

Weigh 50 g of dog biscuits.
How many biscuits are there?
Can you calculate how many you would get
in 500 g?

Division

The child has had experience of sharing into groups using structured apparatus. In this chapter he meets formal division in the abstract using his table book as an aid if necessary.

Care must be taken to ensure that in filling in the answers in the formal operation of division, the digits are placed in the correct column.

Page no.	Content	New language
40	Formal division of Tens and Units by 2, 3, 4, 5, 6, 10 (no remainders)	
41	Formal division of Hundreds, Tens and Units by 2, 3, 4, 5, 6, 10 (with decomposition—no remainders) —with apparatus initially.	

Before doing the work on formal division, please read the comments on page 78 of this book concerning "patters" to be used.

There are more practice examples on page 67 of the Pupils' Book if required.

Further activities

Factor game. Make a pack of cards, each one having a number less than 100, trp 40, 41. One card at a time is turned over, and the first child to give a factor of the number shown (other than the number itself and 1) keeps the card. If the number shown is a prime number, the child who knows this keeps the card.
The Winner is the child with the most cards when the pack is exhausted.

(Could be done as class or small group activity.)

Multiplication check

When the answers have been obtained by calculation the results should be checked by division.

	56	56
	× 8	8)448
	448	

```
Work these out.
56        39        85
x 8       x 7       x 4
_____     _____     _____

_____     _____     _____

74        38        61
x 6       x 5       x9
_____     _____     _____

_____     _____     _____

Now check them by
dividing
```

Area

This chapter develops ideas on finding area by counting squares.

Page no.	Content	New language
42	Finding area by counting squares	area
43	Work with different shapes of the same area	
44–45	Finding approximate areas of irregular shapes by counting	

Work on tessellation, as an introduction to early ideas on area can be found on page 45 of this Handbook.

In the work in this chapter, area is being found by counting squares. Although the squares used happen to be cm squares, this notation is not formally introduced until Book 4.

When finding areas of irregular shapes, discussion will be necessary to decide how to deal with part squares, and how to count the squares systematically (e.g. a row at a time).

Further activities

Find the areas of various shapes.
Either squared paper or transparent grids may be used.
The squared paper may have squares of any suitable size.

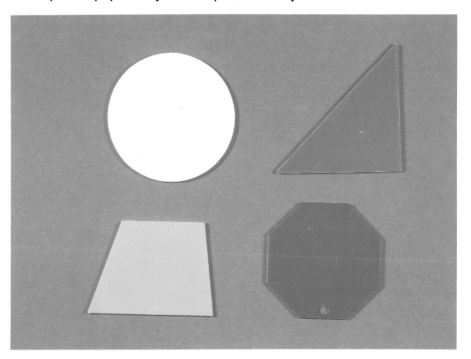

Geoboard activity

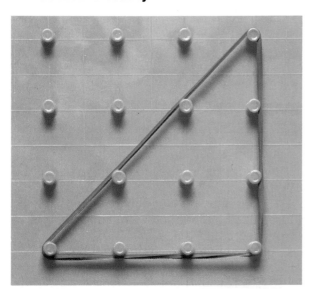

Make a triangle on a 16 pin board.
Find its area.
Make another triangle of the same area.
Repeat for various shapes.
Results can be shown on spotty paper.

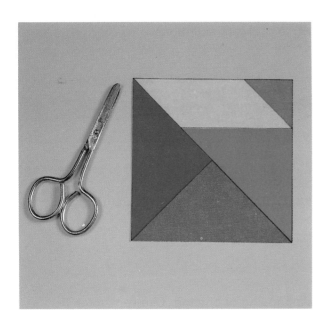

Tangrams *trp* 42.
These can be used for activities on conservation of area. Discussion will be necessary.
Cut up this square and rearrange the pieces to make a triangle.
Make a four-sided shape which is not square (e.g. parallelogram).

What shapes can you make with these six triangles? *trp* 43.
The triangles should be equilateral.

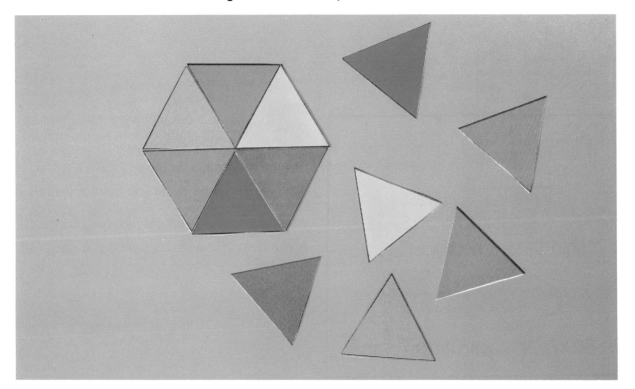

Money

The computational skills involving money previously acquired are now practised and applied to problem situations.

Page no.	Content	New language
46	Addition, subtraction and multiplication of money	
47	Problems	

The skill of "counting on" when giving change needs to be taught as an oral activity.

There are more practice examples on page 68 of the Pupils' Book if required.

Further activities

Realistic situations involving giving of change. Use real coins if possible, but otherwise plastic ones. Child should be encouraged to give change in as few coins as possible. The correct change could be indicated as coins on the back of the card if wished for self-checking—in this case one 5p, 10p and 50p coin respectively.

Which items would you choose if you had £10 to spend? (Child could choose single items or combination of items.)
How much change would you have?

Which three items could you buy for less than £10?
What coins would you get for your change?

Which items have you bought if you get £1·40 change?

Time

All the early work on Time is built around the "minutes past" notation (e.g. 50 minutes past 1). Having established this notation in earlier work, the same notation is now introduced in shortened form and applied to problems.

The oral notation (e.g. 10 to 2) can be dealt with orally or left until it arises in Book 4.

Page no.	Content	New language
48	Introduction of short form of minutes past notation (e.g. 4.15)	
49	Further practice in short form notation and problems	
50	Introduction of a.m.; p.m.	a.m. p.m.
51	Introduction of midday, midnight; problems	midday midnight

Further activities

The work on the T.V. Times (page 51 of the Pupils' Book) could be extended to video recording. Choose programmes to fit on a 2 hour video tape from the T.V. Times.

Worksheet activity

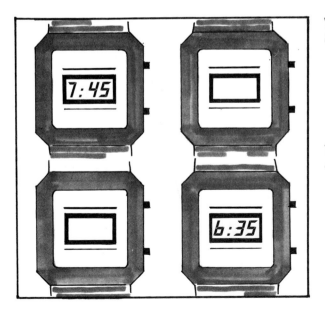

What time will the watch show 40 minutes later?

What time did the watch show 50 minutes earlier?

Graphs

The child has met column graphs with the scale 1:2. This chapter extends this experience to include smaller scales.

In all the graph work so far and in this chapter the information has been so structured that it gives points which fall exactly on the lines cutting the vertical axis.

Page no.	Content	New language
52	Drawing of column graph (scale 1:2)	
53	Interpretation of column graph (scale 1:5)	
54–55	Interpretation of column graph (scale 1:10)	

Further activities

Any subject matter presenting scales to match those done in the Pupils' Book would be suitable. Gathering of random information for graphing can bring difficulties in these early stages of using scales, so it may be wise to offer the information for children to use. Do not forget to ask questions on graphs completed, to give children practice in interpretation.

Suitable subject matter for column graphs (with scales up to 1:10):
   Types of stall on the market (e.g. food, clothes etc.).
   Number of children staying for dinner each day of the week.
   Direction of children's homes from school (using general directions of N S E W, since this should result in a fairly simple scale).

Investigations

Most of the situations presented in this chapter are of an open-ended nature and do not necessarily result in one particular solution for a given problem. The number of solutions and the time spent on each problem are discretionary.

Page no.	Content	New language
56–57	Investigations with tessellating tiles	
58–59	Magic squares	
60	Work on number combinations on an equaliser balance	
61	Work on routes	

The word diagonal is used in the instructions relating to Magic Squares on pages 58 and 59, even though this term has not been previously introduced. Children working with Magic Squares may need some guidance from the teacher; it should be pointed out that no number can be used more than once in a Magic Square.

The washers shown on the equaliser balance on page 60 indicate the pegs on which the washers are to be hung, and not the number of washers on each peg. The child has to discover how many washers need to be placed on each peg shown.

Further activities

a) Magic Squares (pages 58–59)
Once a magic square has been established, further ones can be made by carrying out the same operation on each number in the square (i.e. ×2, or −1 etc.). It is therefore a simple task to prepare other squares for children to work on from those shown in the Pupils' Book.

b) Equaliser balance (page 60)
The child has to decide how many washers are on each peg of the illustration, and balance them by putting washers on the other side of the balance on one peg only.
(2 Washers on 5, 1 on 6. Needs 2 washers on 8 or 8 washers on 2)

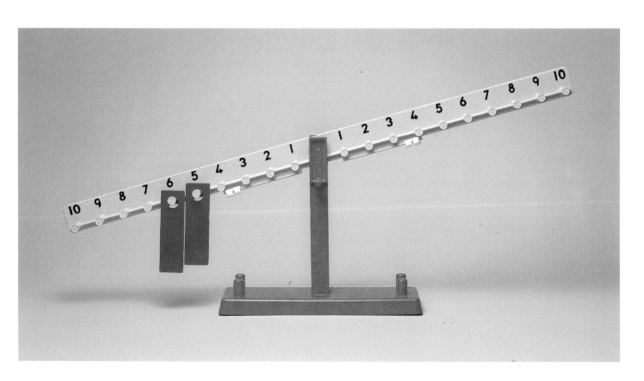

(2 Washers on 9, 2 on 5. Needs 4 washers on 7 or 7 washers on 4)

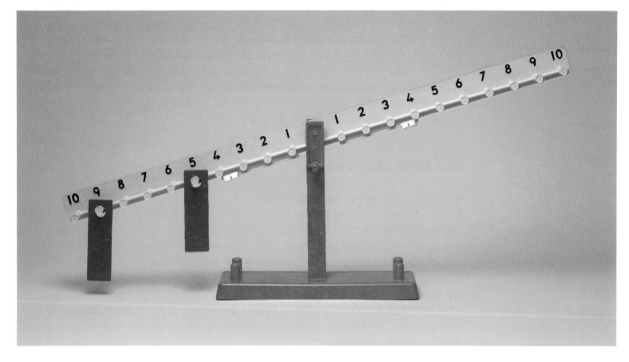

c) Routes (page 61)
For ideas on routes, using geoboards, see the further activities suggested on page 119 of this Handbook.

Problem pages

These pages allow the child to apply the numerical skills, acquired earlier, in a problem situation.

Page no.	Content	New language
62–63	Number and Money problems	

More practice

The "more practice" pages are included for those children for whom the teacher feels extra practice in computational skills is desirable. It may well be that for many children the work on these pages may not be necessary.

The "more practice" pages can also be used, of course, for revision purposes.

Page no.	Content	New language
64	More practice—addition of number	
65	More practice—subtraction of number	
66	More practice—multiplication of Hundreds, Tens and Units	
67	More practice—division of Hundreds, Tens and Units (no remainders)	
68	More practice—addition, subtraction, multiplication of money	
69	More practice—addition, subtraction of m, g	

Assessment (pages 70–71)

The major teaching points are tested in these assessment pages, and they must be completed before going on to the next stage. If mistakes arise in the test, care should be taken that they are not due to a lack of understanding of the concepts and skills involved.

Book 4

The following pages detail the content of each page of Peak Book 4 shown under chapter headings and where appropriate include comments upon specific teaching points. It also suggests, chapter by chapter, further activities which supplement, consolidate or extend the skills being developed.

Addition

The child has now acquired the skills of addition and this chapter gives the opportunity to practise and apply those skills.

Page no.	Content	New language
4	Making numbers up to 100; quick addition of 9	
5	Quick addition of 99	
6	Addition of number	
7	Addition of money, length	
8	Missing numbers	
9	Problems	

Further practice examples are provided on page 66 of the Pupils' Book if required.

Further activities

Crossword type addition puzzle. (Answers shown for information.)

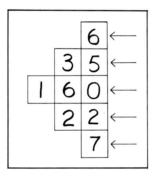

Add the first two even numbers.

Add $\frac{1}{8}$ of 112 to $\frac{1}{3}$ of 63.

Total number of pence in £1·01 and 59p.

What we must add to 19 to make 41.

Add all the factors of 4.

Similar puzzles can be set which concentrate on other operations (or language), or which use a mixture of operations.

Simple cards on structure of number.
The child uses the first example to complete the others without any "working out".
This can be extended to adding 10 to each number, or doubling each number and the consequent effect on the answer.

$$16 + 27 = 43$$
so
$$16 + 37 =$$
$$26 + 27 =$$
$$116 + 27 =$$

18 + 16 = 34
SO
16 + 18 =
34 − 18 =
34 − 16 =

Similar work to the previous cards, but emphasising the relationship between addition and subtraction. Discussion is necessary with the child before he attempts the work—it loses its value if he works the examples out.

Code
A E R S T
2 6 9 1 8

SET
+ SAT
————

Find the word
your answer makes.

Decoding addition sums to produce a word.

An exercise for the more able child which is self-checking.

How much has she spent on food?

Simple addition situations where some of the information is not relevant.
It is important to train children to select information and disregard that which is no use to them.

Length

Measurement of perimeter was introduced in Book 3 and this chapter extends the work to include estimation. Multiplication and division in metre notation are also introduced and applied in a problem situation.

This chapter introduces multiplication and division in metre notation and involves the use of a decimal point. At this stage the decimal point is simply a separator between metres and centimetres and no attempt should be made to explain its function as a true decimal. This will be done in later books.

Further practice examples are provided on page 69 of the Pupils' Book if required.

Further activities

Find the longest route to visit every pin once on a 9 pin geoboard.
There must be no crossings.
Do it with string and measure the distance.
Do the same to find the shortest route.
Do the same with a 16 pin board.

Measure the distance round a piece of paper.
Fold the paper in half.
How far is it round the paper now?
(Is it half the previous distance?)
Halve the paper a different way (e.g. diagonally).
How far is it round the paper now?
(Is it the same as before?)
(Is it half the distance this time?)
Repeat the activity, folding the piece of paper into quarters.

Child makes one jump from a mark on the floor and measures it.
He calculates how far 5 jumps will take him. He makes the jumps and measures. Discuss with the child the reason for the difference in the two results.

Similar activities can be done involving hopping and striding etc.
Child makes 2 marks on playground a distance apart (suggest 15 m).
He makes one jump from the first mark and then has to estimate how many more jumps will be needed to reach the other mark. He can repeat this activity for hops and strides.

Gather a selection of bolts and nuts which fit them. Child measures a bolt and estimates how many complete turns of the nut will take it to the top. (Colour one side of the nut for ease of counting.)
Does length of bolt determine how many turns of the nut are needed to reach the top of the bolt?

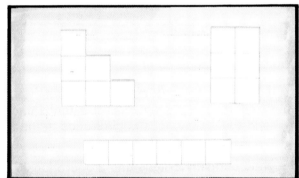

Which combination of six squares gives the greatest perimeter?
Which gives the least perimeter?
Similar activities with other numbers of squares.
Is there a rule?

What is the shortest distance round a cube?
What is the longest distance using 4 straight lines only?

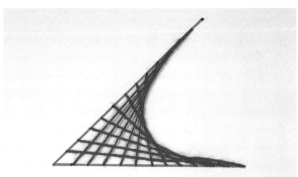

Simple curved stitching activities where the measurements along the axes are an exact number of cm.

Subtraction

The child has acquired all the skills of subtraction involving Thousands, Hundreds, Tens and Units, and this chapter gives further practice and applies them to problem situations.

There are more practice examples on page 66 of the Pupils' Book if required.

Further activities

The child is given 2 digits and 2 operations. He can use them on the calculator as often as he wishes.

He has to reach a given target using only the digits and the operations he has been given. (For instance he has the digits 4 and 5, and the operations of subtraction and multiplication.

He has to reach a target of 21 on the calculator.)

He records his entries on the calculator as:

$$5 - 4 \qquad \times 5 \qquad \times 5 \qquad - 4 = 21$$

Can a partner do it in fewer moves?

441	106
360	205
702	61
414	151
801	43

The digits of each number add up to 9.

The digits of each number add up to 7.

Child subtracts any number in the 2nd column from any number in the 1st column. Add the digits of the answer and continue to do so until you arrive at a single digit.

e.g.

$$\begin{array}{r} 441 \\ -\ 151 \\ \hline 290 \end{array}$$

$2 + 9 + 0 = 11$
$1 + 1 = 2$

$$\begin{array}{r} 360 \\ -\ 205 \\ \hline 155 \end{array}$$

$1 + 5 + 5 = 11$
$1 + 1 = 2$

$$\begin{array}{r} 702 \\ -\ 106 \\ \hline 596 \end{array}$$

$5 + 9 + 6 = 20$
$2 + 0 = 2$

The final answer will remain constant, so long as the digits in each number of the first column add up to a constant number, and similarly in the 2nd column. The same activity applies to addition.

For the very able child an explanation may be attempted, and the child could make up new sets of numbers.

Shape

This chapter extends the range of plane shapes and the terminology of shape.

Further activities

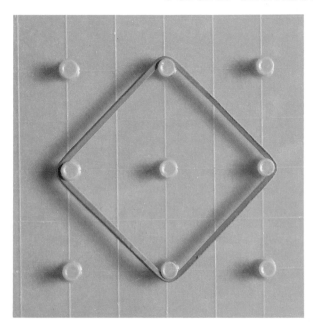

How many different polygons can you make on a 9 pin geoboard?
Each polygon must have a different number of sides.
How many different polygons can you make on a 16 pin geoboard?

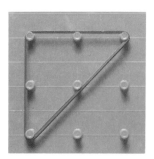

Find as many different triangles as you can on a 9 pin geoboard. (Record on spotty paper.)
Similar activities on a 16 pin geoboard.
With the more able child, discuss whether certain triangles are "different" (i.e. size/shape).

Similar activities with squares.

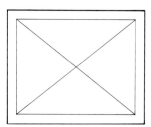

Draw a rectangle.
Draw both diagonals and measure them.
Are they both the same length?
Similar activities with a square.

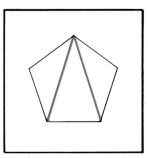

Draw a pentagon.
Draw two diagonals from the same vertex.
Measure them with dividers.
Are they the same length?

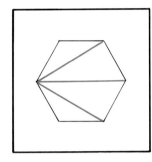

Draw a hexagon.
Draw three diagonals from the same vertex.
Measure them with dividers.
Are they the same length?

Find the centre of a regular shape by folding.
(The folds will not necessarily be diagonals.)

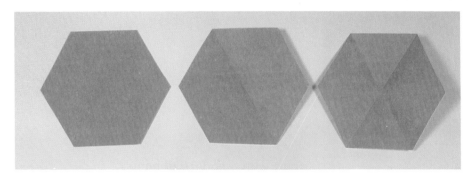

Use geostrips to form irregular shapes.
Draw and label them.

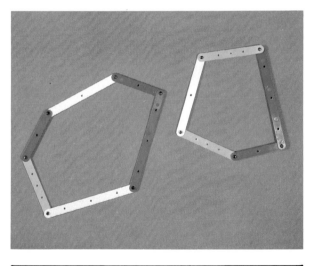

No. of sides	No. of right angles	Length of longest side	Perimeter

Start with a paper rectangle.
Fill in the details of it on the table shown.
Halve the rectangle in any way and fill in the
details of the new shape on the table.
Shape could then be quartered and the
activity repeated.

Using Art straws, make a shape which will hold a cube (or sphere etc.) without it dropping out.

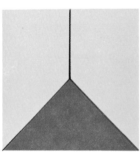

Start with a square of paper.
Colour, or cut out, one piece to leave only one line of symmetry.

Angles

The children are now familiar with the four points of the compass and the right angle. This chapter extends the work to include the eight points of the compass, and a $\frac{1}{2}$ right angle.

Page no.	Content	New language
24	Compass work	NE, NW, SE, SW
25	Work on $\frac{1}{2}$ right angle	

Further activities

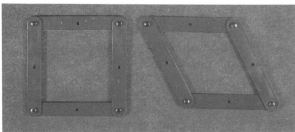

Make a square with geostrips.
Twist the square.
How many angles are there greater than a right angle?
How many less than a right angle?
Alter the shape as often as you wish and re-test.
Similar activities with a rectangle.

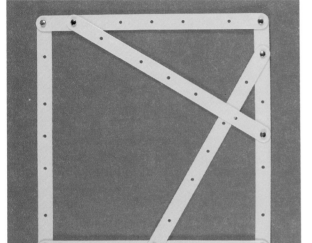

Make a square with geostrips.
Use 2 more strips to create 4 more right angles inside the square.

(Any solution, including the diagonals, or like the one opposite is acceptable.)

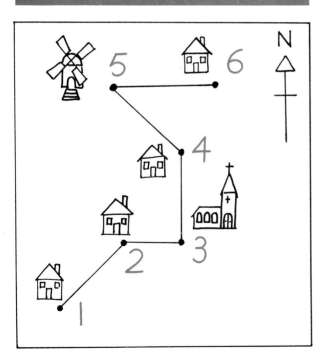

To get from 1 to 6 you must go:

From 1 NE to 2, then E to 3, then N to 4, then NW to 5, then E to 6.

Ask the child to plan the return route.

Multiplication

As all the tables should now be known, this chapter gives further practice in multiplication, and introduces factors.

There are more practice examples on page 67 of the Pupils' Book if required.

Further activities

Number rod activity

Build a cube with 2 rods.
Use as few rods as possible.
How many rods did you need?
Repeat with other sized rods, in order to recognise relationship between size of rod, and number needed to make cube
(i.e. 2 rods, 2×2 needed $= 4$
3 rods, 3×3 needed $= 9$
4 rods, 4×4 needed $= 16$).

How many 3 rods will match 15?
How many 5 rods will match 15?
This activity develops early ideas on factors.

How many 2 rods will match 16?
Say how many 8 rods. Were you right?
Which other rods will match it?

Number puzzle

Write any 3 digit number, where the first digit is the smallest, and the last digit the largest.

```
278
  4
 24
120
127
1270
1278
278
```

1. Take the hundreds digit and double it.
2. Add 20.
3. Multiply by 5.
4. Add the tens digit of the starting number.
5. Multiply by 10.
6. Add the unit digit of the starting number.
7. Subtract 1000.

Will it work with other numbers?

Which digits can be made into 100 by multiplication only?
e.g. 2 ($\times$ 5 $\times$ 10) = 100
    3 (cannot be done)
    4 ($\times$ 5 $\times$ 5) = 100 etc.

Which can be made into 200, 300 etc.?
(Those which can be made into 100 can be made into any multiple of 100.)

For the very able child, which is the lowest multiple of 100 which each digit can be made into, by multiplication.
e.g. 2 ($\times$ 5 $\times$ 10) = 100; 3 ($\times$ 10 $\times$ 10) = 300 etc.
Similar activities with "targets" of 1000.
(Suitable for calculator work.)

Calculator activity   Factor game for two people.
Choose a number to be the factor for the game (e.g. 4).

Child A enters a number which must be less than 100 and not a multiple of 4 (e.g. 45).

Child B then adds or subtracts any number between 1 and 5 to make it a multiple of 4 (e.g. -1).

The answer is then checked by dividing by 4.
Child B now takes his turn to enter a number.

Write numbers with digits that add up to 10.

$$
\begin{array}{r}
163 \\
\times \quad 6 \\
\hline
978
\end{array} \rightarrow 24 \rightarrow 6
$$

Multiply each number by 6.
Find the digital root of your answer.

$$
\begin{array}{r}
208 \\
\times \quad 6 \\
\hline
1248
\end{array} \rightarrow 15 \rightarrow 6
$$

Will this work if you multiply by another number?

Capacity

The child is now familiar with the relationship between litres and millilitres and this chapter introduces litre notation.
   The same comments apply to the decimal point as in metre notation (see page 119).

Page no.	Content	New language
30	Addition of ml; changing to l, ml	
31	Introduction of litre notation, and problems	

Further activities

In the following activities it is suggested that it would be sensible to use plastic semi-transparent containers.
The child could make his own graduated cylinder. Discussion will be necessary to decide how best to do this, and what graduations to use.

Which container holds twice as much as **C**?

A B C D E F

Structure a group of containers, so that one holds twice as much as another; one holds 500 ml more than another etc.
Pose relevant questions, and ask the child to choose before actually measuring.
Discussion may be necessary about the method of measuring.
It will test a child's estimation of capacity more acutely if the plastic containers are different shapes.

How many doses of medicine are in the bottle?

(Doses could vary if you wish.)
How long will it last?

Practical work linking capacity and weight.
Find the weight of 2 flat tablespoonsful of sand.
Find the weight of 2 flat tablespoonsful of rice.
Similar activities based on amounts measured in measuring cylinder or jug.
What will 100 ml of sand weigh?
Calculate the weight of 200 ml of sand.
Check your answer by weighing 200 ml of sand.

Fractions

This chapter extends the child's knowledge of fractions to include eighths and their equivalences with other fractions already introduced.

Further activities

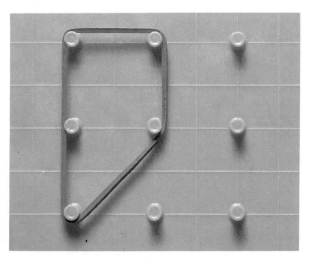

Work has already been done on finding $\frac{1}{2}$ and $\frac{1}{4}$ of a 9 pin geoboard.

This can now be extended to include eighths (and multiples of eighths) on a 9 pin board.

Similar work can be done on other sized boards, and the more able child may find which fractions cannot be made in this way on certain boards.

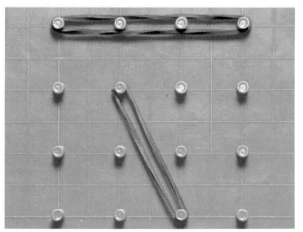

Similar work to the above on a rectangular geoboard (e.g. 3 × 4). Such a board can be made from a 4 × 4 board, by "blanking off" one row of pins with an elastic band.

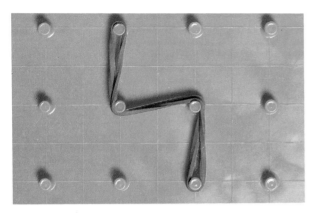

How many ways can you halve a 3 × 4 board?
  a) using neither middle pin?
  b) using one middle pin only?
  c) using both middle pins?
Similar work can be done with other fractions.

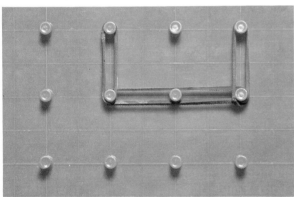

Find as many ways as you can of "chopping off" 2 squares.
Find as many ways as you can of dividing the 3 × 4 board into thirds.

With all these activities involving geoboards, recording can be done on spotty paper.

Fold a piece of paper in half, then fold again, then again. Colour the side facing you.
What fraction of the paper has been coloured?
Open the paper out to check.
Similar activities, asking child to fold paper twice, and colouring only a half of the side facing him.
What fraction has been coloured?

Weight

This chapter introduces the relationship between the kilogram and grams, and also kilogram notation.

The comment on the decimal point in metre notation also applies here (see page 119).

Page no.	Content	New language
38	Introduction of kilogram, kg; weighing in kg	kilogram, kg
39	Addition of g; changing to kg, g; introduction to kg notation	

Further activities

The child needs as much opportunity as possible to weigh selected objects. Combined weights can be calculated and changed into kilogram notation.

Pictures of objects and their weights (in grams) for child to calculate how much two would weigh, or other multiples of the weight. Answers to be changed to kilogram notation.

Reading to be done by child. Cost of posting of parcels (shown in grams) to be shown on a card. Child to decide how much it would cost to send each parcel.

Division

Further practice is given in this chapter in the skills of formal division, and the work done includes remainders for the first time.

There are more practice examples on page 67 of the Pupils' Book if required.

Further activities

Number puzzle:

4712
2741
1971
219

9)1971

Write any 4 digit number.
Rearrange the digits in any way.
Subtract the smaller from the larger.
Divide the answer by 9.
Is there a remainder?
Repeat this a number of times.
(There will never be a remainder.)
Establish rules of exact divisibility by practice and discussion.

(e.g. All even numbers will divide exactly by 2.)

All numbers whose digits add up to a multiple of 3 will divide exactly by 3.
All numbers whose digits add up to a multiple of 9 will divide exactly by 9.
All numbers whose last two digits will divide exactly by 4 are exactly divisible by 4 (relate to leap year).

Try the rules out on the calculator, by putting on display random numbers and deciding what they can be divided by without leaving remainders.

61	55	52	27	34	29	41	37	55	13	52	13	35	25	28	23	11	40
9	41	28	31	65	37	24	61	16	29	46	15	0	12	54	10	37	9
7	37	5	43	35	14	36	7	9	41	33	5	48	18	17	29	40	26
40	14	29	19	23	11	60	22	29	11	34	13	19	25	29	31	61	25
19	49	50	26	32	49	6	24	36	42	48	60	39	50	16	35	7	16
32	53	47	17	53	40	54	36	24	36	42	54	29	38	50	14	40	50
26	17	41	19	35	48	13	10	7	29	35	41	60	41	47	29	8	47
11	35	15	11	54	26	32	44	40	19	8	30	46	54	15	27	39	38

Colour mosaics:
Colour all numbers which are exactly divisible by 6.

Area

The child has had practice in finding area by counting squares, and this chapter introduces the idea of measuring area with a standard unit of square centimetres.

Page no.	Content	New language
44	Introduction of cm² as a standard unit	square centimetre cm²
45	Finding area of shapes in cm²	
46–47	Estimation and measurement of area	

Further activities

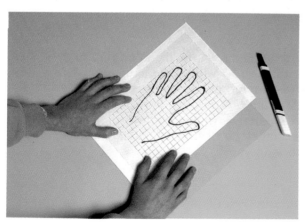

Allow the child as many opportunities as possible of estimating and counting the areas of familiar shapes (e.g. hand, foot, round shapes etc.). A transparent grid (cm²) is needed for the counting.

Using geostrips.
Make different shapes and draw round the inside of each.
Find the areas.

Make a square, or rectangle, then slope the shape.
Does the area change?
The more you slope the shape, what happens to the area? (It reduces)
When do you get the largest area?

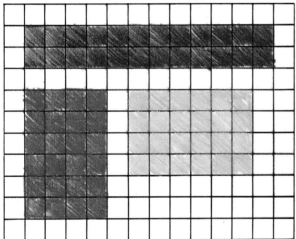

On cm squared paper, draw as many different rectangles as you can with an area of 24 cm².

Also refer to the activities in the Fractions section on page 132, which are based on area.

Money

Practice is given here in the computational skills involving money, and these skills are applied to problem situations.

Page no.	Content	New language
48	Addition, subtraction, multiplication, division of money	
49–51	Problems	

Page 48 Care should be taken in the division of money to ensure that the digits in the answer are written in the correct column.
There are more practice examples on page 68 of the Pupils' Book if required.

Further activities

Any activities which involve the child in "handling money", whether practically or computationally, are useful, together with any experiences which are based on equivalence of coins.

Bills, transactions involving change, making up to £1, work on pocket money (graphs), admission charges, school tuck shops, money raised at school functions, rides at the fair, bus fares, the cost of holidays; all these are situations which are meaningful to a child.

Time

Having introduced the shortened form of the "minutes past" notation (e.g. 2.40) this chapter deals with the oral form of time telling (e.g. 10 to 2). We suggest that it may be sensible to do this as a class or group activity.

Page no.	Content	New language
52–53	Introduction of minutes past/minutes to notation	

Further activities

The work outlined in this chapter can also be followed up as an ongoing activity with a class or group, with any work concerned with telling the time. Small amounts of work done fairly frequently and incidentally are better than a whole block of further activities.

Further activities on time fall into three categories:
a) Work concerned with oral telling of time (e.g. quarter to 4).
b) Work concerned with written form of time (e.g. 3.45 p.m.).
c) Activities and problems concerned with passage of time (e.g. length of T.V. programmes, time taken to travel from A to B, things that can be done in, say, one minute).

Graphs

The child should now be fully familiar with column graphs, and during this chapter he will meet a variety of scales.

You will see from the graphs and table of information that the part squares used in some columns are always $\frac{1}{4}$, $\frac{1}{2}$, or $\frac{3}{4}$ of a full square, with scales to suit the situation.

Page no.	Content	New language
54–55	Interpretation of column graph (scale 1 : 4) —columns including part squares	
56	Interpretation of column graph (scale 1 : 20) —columns including part squares	
57	Drawing of column graph (scale 1 : 100) —columns including part squares	

Further practice

Any subject matter which is suitable to be represented as a column graph could be used for further practice. Care should be taken that the information given to the child for graphing does not cause problems for him in selecting suitable scales. The child needs practice in both drawing and interpreting graphs. If he is allowed to gather information in a random way for graphing, then he will need a lot of advice in deciding scales, or he may run into unforeseen difficulties.

Suitable subject matter for column graphs (with scales):
Favourite football teams, pop stars, lessons, types of book, colours of jumpers, etc.
Visitors to cinema, exhibition, fair etc. in a week.
Types of swimming certificates, gymnastic certificates won in school in a year.

Investigations

Most of the situations presented in this chapter are of an open-ended nature and do not necessarily result in one particular solution for a given problem. The number of solutions and the time spent on each problem are discretionary.

Page no.	Content	New language
58–59	Investigation of digital patterns	digit
60–61	Square numbers	square numbers
62	Work with pentominoes	pentomino
63	Work with hexominoes	hexomino

Further activities

a) Digital roots investigation (page 59)
The patterns which evolve are as follows:
2 × table—even numbers followed by odd numbers
(2, 4, 6, 8, 1, 3, 5, 7, 9)
4 × table—alternating numbers decrease by one
(4, 8, 3, 7, 2, 6; 1, 5, 9: repeating)
5 × table—alternating numbers increase by one
(5, 1, 6, 2, 7, 3 etc.)
6 × table—6, 3, 9 repeating
7 × table—decreasing odd numbers, followed by decreasing
even numbers (7, 5, 3, 1, 8, 6, 4, 2 etc.)
8 × table—8, 7, 6, 5, 4 etc.
9 × table—9, 9, 9, repeating
10 × table—1, 2, 3, 4 etc.

b) Square numbers (pages 60–61)
Similar work can be done with "L" numbers as follows:

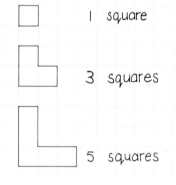

1 square

3 squares

5 squares

The "L" shape numbers are all the odd numbers.
If they are put together they make the square numbers.

This illustrates that: $4 = 3 + 1$
$9 = 5 + 3 + 1$
$16 = 7 + 5 + 3 + 1$

i.e. square numbers are made by addition of consecutive odd numbers.

c) Pentominoes (pages 62–63)
This work can be developed into work on perimeter (see further activities in Length on page 121).

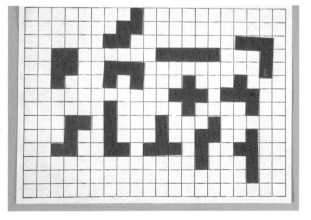

Which combination of 5 squares gives the maximum/minimum number of vertices?
Which of the pentominoes you have made can be folded into an open box?
For the very able child—can you put all the different pentominoes together to make a rectangle?

Similar work can be done with pentominoes and hexominoes based on an equilateral triangle.

Problem pages

These pages allow the child to apply the numerical skills, acquired earlier, in a problem situation.

Page no.	Content	New language
64–65	Problems involving length	

More practice

The "more practice" pages are included for those children for whom the teacher feels extra practice in computation skills is desirable. It may well be that for many children the work on these pages may not be necessary.

The "more practice" pages can also be used, of course, for revision purposes.

Page no.	Content	New language
66	More practice—addition, subtraction of number	
67	More practice—multiplication, division of number	
68	More practice—money	
69	More practice—measurement	

Assessment (pages 70–71)

The major teaching points are tested in these assessment pages, and they must be completed before going on to the next stage. If mistakes arise in the test, care should be taken that they are not due to a lack of understanding of the concepts and skills involved.

Apparatus list Books 0–4

Book no.	Equipment required		Types of paper
0	Number line Base 10 M.A.B. materials place value sheet		
1	tape measure straws Base 10 M.A.B. materials place value sheet cup, jar, beaker, bottle, dish, funnel peas, marbles, beads, counters, bottle tops coins	clock stamp plane shapes solid shapes litre jug balance, weights 9 pin geoboard elastic bands Cuisenaire or Stern rods	gummed circles gummed squares squared paper spotty paper
2	Base 10 M.A.B. materials place value sheet tape measure clock face clock stamp beaker board rubber metre stick dice	plane shapes solid shapes litre, $\frac{1}{2}$ litre, $\frac{1}{4}$ litre jugs balance, weights 9 pin geoboard elastic bands pegboards pegs	squared paper spotty paper
3	set square milk bottle, jam jar Base 10 M.A.B. materials clock stamp	mirror plane shapes graduated cylinder equaliser balance	paper circle squared paper card
4	transparent cm² grid clock stamp tape, trundle wheel bean bags plane shapes	16 pin geoboard, elastic bands compass balance, weights bathroom scales pegboard, pegs	gummed circles spotty paper squared paper isometric paper

Cumulative vocabulary list

Number

General		Subtraction / Addition / Multiplication	Division / Fractions
General	least	count on	groups
abacus/abaci	less than	equals	lots of
as many as	match	plus	multiply
behind	middle	together	sets of
ordinal numbers (names of)	more than	total	table square
dice	most		
digit	next to	**Subtraction**	**Division**
enough	odd	count back	divide
even	ordinal numbers (names of)	difference	half
few	pentomino	leaves	halve
fewer	rods	left	remainder
fewest	spotty paper	minus	share
finish	start	subtract	
geoboard	the same as	subtraction	**Fractions**
greater than	too many	take away	eighth ($\frac{1}{8}$)
hexomino			half ($\frac{1}{2}$)
how many?	**Addition**	**Multiplication**	one-third ($\frac{1}{3}$)
in front of	add	double	quarter ($\frac{1}{4}$)
last	altogether	factor	three-quarters ($\frac{3}{4}$)
			two-thirds ($\frac{2}{3}$)

Time

after	half past	next	same time
afternoon	hour	night-time	seasons (names of)
a.m.	hour hand	o'clock	slow
before	late	past	special days (names of)
days (names of)	midday	p.m.	today
day time	midnight	quarter past	tomorrow
early	minute	quarter to	year
evening	months (names of)	quick	yesterday
fast	morning		

Measurement (where comparatives and superlatives apply, these have not been stated)

Capacity			
Capacity	container	full	litre (l)
amount	deep	holds less	millilitre (ml)
arbitrary units (names of)	empty	holds more	narrow
capacity	estimate	level	pour

shallow
wide

Length
arbitrary units (names of)
big
breadth
centimetre (cm)
fat
height

high
just over
just under
large
length
long
low
metre (m)
narrow
nearly

short
small
tall
thick
thin
wide

Weight
arbitrary units (names of)
balance
kilogram (kg), gram (g)

heavy
just over
just under
light
nearly
weighs more/less
weights

Area
area
square centimetre (cm²)

Money

altogether
amount
bill
buy
cash

change
cheap
coins (names of)
dear
heads

less
more
pence
penny
pound (£)

sell
shop
spend
tails
value
worth

Shape

circle
cone
corner
cover
cube
cuboid
curved
cylinder
diagonal
diameter
dull
edge
equilateral triangle
face

fit together
flat
gaps
hexagon
hollow
octagon
overlap
pentagon
perimeter
plane
rectangle
roll
rough
semi-circle

shape
shiny
side
slide
smooth
solid
spaces
sphere
square
straight
surface
symmetry (line of)
tessellate
triangle

triangular prism
vertex (vertices)

Angles
anti-clockwise
clockwise
compass
east
north
right angle
south
set square
west

Graphs

arrow graph
column graph

horizontal axis

picture graph

vertical axis